D0858315

Classics In
Child Development

Classics In Child Development

MEASUREMENT
OF INTELLIGENCE BY
DRAWINGS

Florence L. Goodenough

ARNO PRESS

A New York Times Company

New York — 1975

Reprint Edition 1975 by Arno Press Inc.

Reprinted from a copy in
  The University of Illinois Library

Classics in Child Development
ISBN for complete set: 0-405-06450-0
See last pages of this volume for titles.

Manufactured in the United States of America

———◆———

Library of Congress Cataloging in Publication Data

Goodenough, Florence Laura.
    Measurement of intelligence by drawings.

    (Classics in child development)
    Reprint of the ed. published by World Book Co.,
Yonkers-on-Hudson, N. Y., in series: Measurement and
adjustment series.
    Bibliography: p.
    1. Mental tests. 2. Draw-a-man test. 3. Child
study. I. Title. II. Series. Series: Measurement
and adjustment series.
BF431.G628 1975   155.4'18   74-21410
ISBN 0-405-06462-4

MEASUREMENT AND
ADJUSTMENT SERIES
EDITED BY LEWIS M. TERMAN

MEASUREMENT OF INTELLIGENCE BY DRAWINGS

BY FLORENCE L. GOODENOUGH, PH.D.

Research Assistant Professor
Institute of Child Welfare
University of Minnesota

Yonkers-on-Hudson, New York
WORLD BOOK COMPANY
2126 Prairie Avenue, Chicago
1926

WORLD BOOK COMPANY

THE HOUSE OF APPLIED KNOWLEDGE

Established 1905 by Caspar W. Hodgson

YONKERS-ON-HUDSON, NEW YORK
2126 PRAIRIE AVENUE, CHICAGO

A means of measuring the intelligence of children, which would not involve the use of language, has for several years been a desideratum. This book describes a method for measuring intelligence by means of drawings. It illuminates a part of the field of measurement and adjustment concerning which little has previously been known

MAS : GMID–1

PREFACE

THE experiment about to be described was undertaken with the object of determining the extent to which the nature of the drawings made by children in their early years is conditioned by their intellectual development. Previous investigations have suggested that these drawings may afford a valuable index to the nature and organization of the child's mental processes, and may thus throw light on some of the characteristics of mental growth. The studies which have been made up to the present time do not, however, furnish us with an objective means for rating these characteristics, or for differentiating between those due to intelligence and those due to other factors. The greater number of them were made in connection with the child study movement which reached its height between 1895 and 1915. Intelligence testing was then a new and comparatively undeveloped field, and statistical methods for the treatment of data were used but little. In spite of these limitations, the early investigators were able to show rather conclusively that the drawings made by young children have an intellectual rather than an æsthetic origin. They are determined by concept development rather than by visual imagery or by manual skill. The truth of the saying that "a child draws what he knows, rather than what he sees," has been verified by repeated experimentation.

It has therefore seemed worth while to undertake an investigation of the intellectual factors shown in children's drawings. Such a study, it was believed, might prove to be especially useful in the analysis of mental ability and in the study of race, sex, and individual differences. In order to carry out an investigation of this kind, it was necessary first to construct a scale for measuring intelligence as shown in drawing. For this purpose drawings of the human figure

iii

have been found to be most suitable.   By means of objective analysis and comparison of the drawings of several thousand children of different ages and varying educational achievement, a method of scoring has been derived which has proved serviceable as a measure of general intellectual maturity. The non-verbal nature of the test makes it particularly suitable for studying the mentality of children from foreign homes, and of deaf children.

The results obtained with the test indicate that its validity and reliability are about equal to the validity and reliability of most of the primary group tests in common use.   It is believed that it affords a means for the study of mental development from an angle which has heretofore been disregarded by workers in the field of mental measurement.

Expressions of appreciation are due to the many public school teachers and principals who have contributed material for this study.   Grateful acknowledgments should be made particularly to Miss Alice M. Mehleis, supervisor of primary grades, and Mr. Royal C. Predmore, principal, of Schools Nos. 4 and 10 of Perth Amboy, New Jersey, through whose coöperation the major part of the preliminary experimentation was made possible.   The writer is especially indebted to Professor Lewis M. Terman of Leland Stanford Jr. University, under whose direction the study was completed, for his unfailing interest and helpful criticism.

Florence L. Goodenough

CONTENTS

TABLES

EDITOR'S INTRODUCTION

IN *Measurement of Intelligence by Drawings*, Dr. Goodenough has made important contributions both to psychometrics and to the psychology of child development. Although children's drawings have been made the subject of many investigations during the last forty years (*vide* the 192 selected bibliographical references at the end of this volume), the study by Dr. Goodenough is the first one to apply to this problem the modern techniques which have been developed for the quantitative treatment of objective psychological data. It is this fact, largely, which gives her results such large significance for genetic psychology as well as for mental measurement. Nowhere in psychological literature does one find a better illustration of the rewards which await the investigator who is willing to subject his data to a minute and painstaking analysis. The larger differences between the drawings of young and of older children had been familiar to us for two generations, but it remained for Dr. Goodenough to show how the analysis of small differences could be carried so much farther as to offer a serviceable measure of the general level of mental development. Her entire book constitutes an eloquent sermon on the *significance of the little* in mental test performances.

The author makes no claim to having carried her analysis of small differences to its ultimate limit. Just as it is conceivable that a complete knowledge of the pertinent physiological facts would enable us to infer with certainty the sex and the approximate age of a subject from a single blood cell, so it is conceivable that more complete knowledge of the almost microscopic peculiarities that characterize the drawings of children of each sex and of the various levels of intelligence would enable us to go beyond the accomplishment of Dr. Goodenough. It is hoped that her contribution will in this respect serve as an encouraging stimulus to others who are working in the field of mental measurement.

The author's thoroughgoing acquaintance with the results of others' investigations of children's drawings has not blinded her to the importance of open-minded empirical procedure. The scoring system she has devised does not rest upon either theoretical considerations or the generalizations handed down from preceding investigations. It is founded instead upon the empirical analysis of many thousands of performances by children of both sexes and of every stage of mental development from two to fifteen years.

The Goodenough Intelligence Scale can be briefly characterized as follows:

1. It utilizes nothing but the child's single drawing of a man.

2. It is accordingly non-verbal.

3. It requires no more than ten minutes for testing an entire class, plus about two minutes per child for scoring.

4. It is useful chiefly with children from mental age 4 to mental age 10.

5. Its reliability for a single unselected age group in this range lies between .80 and .90.

6. For separate age groups in the same range it yields an average correlation of .76 with the Stanford Revision of the Binet Scale.

This constitutes a notable accomplishment. As every psychologist knows, the devising of a purely non-verbal intelligence scale offers peculiar difficulties. The majority of such scales either rate very low in reliability and validity or else they are tediously long to administer and cumbersome to score. It is the editor's opinion that the Goodenough Scale, both in reliability and validity, compares favorably with any group test, whether non-verbal or verbal, that has been devised for use in the kindergarten and first two grades. With respect to convenience and economy of time it is in a class quite by itself.

The author does not claim that her scale can satisfactorily take the place of individual tests of the type of the Stanford or Herring Binet. It will, however, prove extremely useful for general surveys and tentative classifications. In the case of many children from foreign homes its results will be found even more valid than those of a Binet test. Rather surprisingly, it appears that scores earned on the Goodenough Scale are not very easily influenced by the ordinary school instruction in drawing, and that the results of specific coaching are not very persistent.

One who would use the drawing test of intelligence should not be satisfied to master merely the directions for administration and scoring. A thorough study of the entire book, with special emphasis on Chapters I and IV, should precede. An acquaintance with the test should become a part of the standard equipment of teachers in the kindergarten and primary grades.

Lewis M. Terman

PART ONE

MEASUREMENT OF INTELLI-
GENCE BY DRAWINGS

CHAPTER ONE

HISTORICAL SURVEY

THE idea that the spontaneous drawings of young children may throw light upon the psychology of child development is not a new one. As early as 1885 Ebenezer Cooke (*28*) [1] published an article on children's drawings in which he described the successive stages of development as he had observed them, and urged that art instruction in the schools be made to conform more nearly to the mentality and interests of the child. Cooke's article attracted much attention and had a decided influence upon educational practice.

In 1887 Corrado Ricci (*96*) published an account of the drawings of a group of Italian children whom he observed during a summer's vacation. Ricci's collection of children's drawings is probably the earliest of which we have a published account.[2]

With the growth of the child study movement a number of similar investigations were undertaken. Perez (*91*), Sully (*114*, *115*), Barnes (*7, 8, 9*), Baldwin (*130*), Shinn (*106*), Brown (*17*), Clark (*24*), Herrick (*44*), Lukens (*70*), Maitland (*74*), O'Shea (*83–85*), and Götze (*36*) are among the best known of the earlier writers on the subject. Their reports are chiefly descriptive, although in some cases a few percentages are included. Nevertheless, their findings are very instructive and have thrown much light upon the workings of children's minds.

The scientific interest in children's drawings reached its

---

[1] The numbers in parentheses refer to entries in the Bibliography at the end of the book (pages 163–173).

[2] An English translation of the main part of Ricci's article may be found in Volume 3 of the *Pedagogical Seminary*.

greatest height between 1900 and 1915. During this period
two great international research undertakings were carried
out. The first of these was conducted according to a plan
proposed by Lamprecht (*144*), and was based largely upon
the method used by Earl Barnes in this country. Drawings
were to be made according to standardized directions by
children from all parts of the world and of all levels of cul-
ture. These drawings were to be sent in to a central bureau
at Leipzig for examination and comparison. Lamprecht's
proposal was received with much enthusiasm, and many
thousands of drawings were sent to him. Almost every
nation in the world was represented. The collection also
included drawings made by several primitive African races.
It is greatly to be regretted that this investigation, which
held such possibilities for psychology, anthropology, and
ethnology, as well as for practical education, has not been
carried through to completion. Levinstein (*62*), who col-
laborated with Lamprecht, has published a summary of
certain parts of the material, but no adequate comparative
study of the entire collection has appeared.

In 1907 Claparède (*23*) outlined a plan for the study of
children's drawings which was quite similar to that by Lamprecht but which had a somewhat different end in view.
Lamprecht was interested primarily in the question of racial
similarities and differences, with special reference to the theory of recapitulation. Claparède proposed a careful study
of the developmental stages in drawing, with the idea of
ascertaining what relationship, if any, exists between aptitude
in drawing and general intellectual ability as indicated by
school work. Claparède's plan was adopted by Ivanoff (*51*)
in a study of the drawings of school children in four Swiss
cantons. Ivanoff worked out a method of scoring the drawings according to a six-point scale which took into consideration (*a*) sense of proportion, (*b*) imaginative conception, and

(c) technical and artistic value — equal weight being given to each of the three criteria. He then compared the obtained values with teachers' ratings for general ability, standing in each of the school subjects, and certain moral and social traits. He found a positive correlation in nearly all instances.

Ivanoff's study was much the most extensive of those based on Claparède's plan. The material which he collected was used also by Katzaroff (56) in a study of the subjects most frequently drawn by children. Katzaroff's results show fair agreement with those obtained by Maitland (74) in this country, although it is impossible to make more than a rough comparison, as Katzaroff did not treat the different ages separately. Maitland found the human figure the most popular subject at all ages up to ten years. In Katzaroff's table it ranks third, with " miscellaneous objects " and " houses " taking first and second places. Katzaroff's subjects ranged in age from six to fourteen years.

Schuyten (105), in a study which extended over a period of several years, made use of a method which differs very materially from those employed by other investigators of his time. His object was to establish, if possible, a standard of excellence for each age — that is, a series of age norms. He used the human figure as the subject. The drawings were made from memory; the children were simply told to draw a man " in whatever way they were accustomed to draw it." By means of very minute measurements of each of the separate parts of the body and by comparison with classic standards, Schuyten hoped to be able to devise an objective method for his ratings. The plan was not successful, but the idea is worthy of note as one of the earliest attempts to devise a purely objective measuring scale based upon age standards.[1]

---

[1] Schuyten's original article is written in Dutch and has never been translated, but an excellent review and criticism will be found in Rouma's *Le Langage Graphique de l'Enfant*, pages 14–17 and 80–83.

Schuyten's method was used by Lobsien (*66*) in a study of drawings made by public school children at Kiel. Although no precise norms were established, he found, as did Schuyten, that with increasing age the proportions of the different parts of the body as drawn by children approach more nearly to the classic standards. Lobsien also compared the drawings of imbeciles with those of normal children and found that, age for age, the sense of proportion displayed by imbeciles is decidedly below that of normal children.

One of the most extensive and carefully controlled studies which has ever been made in this field was that carried on by Kerschensteiner (*57*) at Munich during the years 1903–1905. Kerschensteiner was given the task of reorganizing the course of study in drawing for the folk schools of that city. In order to establish a scientific basis for his work, he spent about two years in the collection and study of almost 100,000 drawings made under standardized conditions by children in Munich and in the surrounding towns and villages. He classified these drawings under three main heads, with certain intermediate types. The main types were as follows:

1. Purely schematic drawings. These correspond to what Verworn has called the " ideoplastic stage " in drawing.

2. Drawing according to visual appearance — the "physicoplastic stage."

3. A still later stage in which the child attempts to give an impression of three-dimensional space.

The book is profusely illustrated and contains many tables showing, by grades and sexes separately, the percentages of children whose drawings fall within each of the three classes mentioned above. The author also devotes several pages to an account of the drawings of three especially gifted boys. He analyzes the differences between the drawings made by the feeble-minded and those by normal children.

and shows that these differences are qualitative as well as quantitative. Not only do the feeble-minded tend to produce drawings which are more primitive than those made by normal children, but their drawings also show lack of coherence — "*Zusammenhangenlosigkeit.*" This difference has been remarked upon by several other writers as well — most recently by Cyril Burt (*19*), who feels that it is possible in most instances to differentiate between the drawings of normal and backward children by this characteristic alone.

Kerschensteiner finds very marked differences between the performances of the two sexes. The boys exceed the girls in all types of drawing except certain kinds of decorative design, in which the girls do better than the boys.

Lena Partridge (*89*) made a study of the frequency with which children of different ages draw the various parts of the human figure, as arms, neck, feet, etc. Certain parts of her tables are reproduced on page 35, for comparison with the results of this study.

Stern (*109–112*) has published several articles on children's drawings and has devoted a chapter to the subject in his book, *Psychologie der frühen Kindheit.* In the *Zeitschrift für angewandte Psychologie*, 1907, he gives an account of the attempts of elementary school children to illustrate the poem "Schlarassenland." Stern calls attention to the differences in imaginative conception displayed by the children, and to the age development in the manner of indicating space.

Probably the most extensive and valuable single study that has ever been made on the subject of children's drawings is that by Rouma (*97*), which included the six divisions indicated below.

I. The drawings made by eight children during a period of nine months were subjected to analysis. These children came from well-to-do homes and ranged in age from seven to eleven years.

II. A group experiment was carried out over a period of ten months, in which specified objects were drawn under Rouma's direct personal supervision by all the members of a school for retarded children and by normal children of both sexes in several schools.

III. During a period of ten months, half an hour a week was devoted to observation of the free drawings made by a class of forty children of from six to eight years of age.

IV. Six half-hour periods a week were devoted to observation of the drawings made by a class of thirty subnormal children ranging in age from nine to eleven years.

V. Daily observation was made of the drawings of children in a special observation class in one of the schools in Brussels.

VI. In addition to these direct observations, drawings from several kindergartens and primary schools were collected for Rouma by the teachers, on the basis of which he selected certain children from these classes for individual study.

Rouma did not employ statistical methods in the treatment of his data, but he bases his conclusions upon unusually careful observations and gives numerous case studies in support of his statements. The book is profusely illustrated.

In his study of the development of drawings of the human figure Rouma distinguishes the following stages:

I. The preliminary stage.

    1. Adaptation of the hand to the instrument.

    2. The child gives a definite name to the incoherent lines which he traces.

    3. The child announces in advance that which he intends to represent.

    4. The child sees a resemblance between the lines obtained by chance and certain objects.

II. Evolution of the representation of the human figure.

    1. First tentative attempts at representation, similar to
        the preliminary stages.

    2. The " tadpole " stage.

    3. Transitional stage.

    4. Complete representation of the human figure as seen
        in full face.

    5. Transitional stage between full face and profile.

    6. The profile.

Rouma states that the drawings of subnormal children
resemble those of younger normal children. He notes, however (page 199), the following special differences between
the two types of drawings :

The spontaneous drawings of subnormal children show : (1) a
marked tendency to automatism, (2) slowness in the evolution from
stage to stage, and (3) frequent retrogression to an inferior stage.
(4) There are numerous manifestations of the flight of ideas. The
drawings which cover a sheet of paper are not finished, and they
have to do with a number of very disparate subjects.   (5) Certain
drawings by subnormal children, taken singly, are very complete ;
but when we examine them more closely we find that the child has
confined himself to a series of sketches which have evolved slowly,
and by slight modifications have gradually reached a certain degree
of perfection. The conservative tendency of the child has favored
the development of the drawing. It occasionally happens that a
subnormal child possesses an unusual power of visual memory and
is thus capable of producing very remarkable drawings. These
cases are analogous to those of other inferiors who display a great
superiority of one of their faculties, of whom Inaudi and Diamondi
are celebrated types. (6) Many subnormal children show a great
anxiety to represent an idea in its totality, or to reproduce all the
details in a given sketch. It is this tendency, above all others,
which favors the perfection of the drawings mentioned in the preceding paragraph. (7) Subnormal children prefer those drawings
in which the same movement frequently recurs, and (8) they do
meticulous work.

We have several very good accounts of the drawings made
by individual children during early childhood. The monograph published by Brown (*17*) includes four studies of this
sort, each extending over a period of from one to three years.
Mrs. Hogan's account of the drawings made by her little son
(*46*) is very complete, but gives the impression of being somewhat colored by maternal pride. Clara and William Stern
(*108*) preserved the drawings made by their son during his
childhood, and also kept a record of the circumstances under
which each was made. Less complete accounts will be found
in many of the well-known child biographies, such as those
by Preyer (*95*), Darwin (*29*), and others.

Unquestionably the best of these individual studies is that
by Luquet (*72*). Luquet preserved every drawing made by
his little daughter, no matter how crude, from the time when
she first began to draw at the age of three years and three
months, up to eight and one half years. During this time
great care was taken to keep the child's drawings free, not
only from adult influence, but also from the influence of other
children. Each drawing was numbered and dated, and the
circumstances under which it was made were noted, together
with the child's comments at the time of drawing, and any
other significant facts. In all, about fifteen hundred drawings were made during this period, a large number of which
are reproduced in Luquet's book.

Luquet shows that a child's drawings undergo much fluctuation from day to day; that a new feature which has once
been shown does not invariably appear thereafter, but that
an appreciable period of time usually elapses before the new
characteristics become fixed in a drawing. For this reason,
and because of the difficulty of interpreting all the elements
in a drawing, he concludes that this is a type of performance
which should not be subjected to statistical treatment. His
study is particularly valuable since it is the only one that

includes all the drawings made by a child over any considerable period of time.

Three other types of study deserve mention. The first
has to do with special talent in drawing, of which the best
example is that made by Kik (*58*) in 1908. Kik observed
the development of thirteen children who appeared to be
especially gifted in drawing. Three of these children had
previously been studied by Kerschensteiner (*57*). Kik
emphasizes the difference between real creative ability and
mere ability to copy. He shows that his cases whose work
indicated this higher type of ability also ranked high in their
general school work, but that the copyists, on the whole, did
rather inferior school work. A more recent study of this
sort, based upon standardized tests, has been made by
Manuel (*76*). Nineteen subjects, ranging from fifth grade
to university students, were given a number of tests designed
to measure both general ability and certain specific types of
ability. The method of selecting the subjects is open to
criticism, since the criterion used appears to have been the
opinion of a single judge, usually the art instructor, although
in several cases the selection seems to have been made by
Manuel. Since the population from which the selection was
made was relatively small, it is not likely that the subjects
who were chosen represent a very high degree of special
artistic ability. The statistical treatment of the data also
leaves much to be desired. Results have been summarized
by individuals and not by tests, deviations are given in terms
of raw score without transformation into comparable units;
and no allowance has been made, either for intercorrelations
between tests or for variations in the intellectual development of the different subjects. His conclusions are suggestive, but they appear to be based more largely upon *a priori*
opinion than upon the objective results of the experiment.

A type of investigation which should richly repay further

work has to do with the drawings made by psychopathic subjects. It is possible that such drawings, if rightly understood, would help to throw light upon the causes of mental disorders and be of material aid in diagnosis. A beginning in this field was made by Reja (*128*) and Rogues de Fursac (*123*). Rouma published an account of the drawings of a subject addicted to pathological lying (*129*). More recent studies have been made by Kurbitz (*125*) and Hamilton (*124*).

The literature of children's drawings abounds in comparisons between the drawings of modern children and those made by prehistoric man or by primitive races of the present day. The study by Lamprecht has already been mentioned. Probst (*145*) has described the drawings made by children of an Algerian tribe which had not been subjected to European influence; Degallier (*134*) observed the drawings made by a small group of Congo negro children; Haddon (*139*), those made by natives of British New Guinea. Comparisons between children's drawings and those of prehistoric races have been made by Van Gennep (*152*), Döhleman (*135*), Verworn (*153*), Kretzschmar (*142, 143*), Grosse (*137*), Rouma (*97*), and others. There is little agreement either in their points of view or in their conclusions. Those who incline toward the theory of recapitulation usually emphasize the primitive nature of both types of drawings and their common failure to represent space. Kretzschmar, especially, calls attention to the latter point. Others, among whom may be mentioned Verworn and Rouma, believe that the resemblances which exist are more apparent than real.

It is obvious that no really valid comparison can be made between the paper and pencil drawings of the modern child and those which prehistoric man smeared on rock walls with a finger dipped in wet clay, or carved out by means of a piece of flint. Moreover, we have no way of knowing what purpose these prehistoric drawings were intended to serve. A carefully executed piece of work which is intended to be an accurate representation of a given object is a very different thing from the hasty sketches which are frequently made by way of giving point to an idea or merely for amusement. We have no reason for believing that the specimens of prehistoric art which have chanced to be preserved are, in all cases, the best which prehistoric man produced, and there is still less ground for the assumption that he could have done no better if he had been provided with the tools which are at the disposal of the modern child. When, in addition to these factors, we consider the unknown but probably very great influence that is exerted upon the drawings of present-day children by the pictures found everywhere in their environment, the uncertain ground which underlies even the most tentative comparison between work done under such widely disparate circumstances becomes evident.

Great caution is also necessary in making comparisons between the drawings of American or European children and those of modern primitive races. However, the difficulties in this case are perhaps not insurmountable. Rouma has shown that while children who have had no experience in drawing do not draw as well in the beginning as their general ability would justify us in expecting, yet a comparatively small amount of practice is sufficient to equalize the factor of experience, so that their drawings soon come to resemble those of other children of their age. The experiments presently to be described bear out this conclusion. Accordingly, a comparison between the drawings made by civilized children and those made by children of primitive races who have spent several months in a mission school where they have had plenty of opportunity to use pencil and paper and to look at pictures is perhaps not grossly unfair.

A comparison of the findings of the investigators whose

work has been described appears to justify the following conclusions:

1. In young children a close relationship is apparent between concept development as shown in drawing, and general intelligence.

2. Drawing, to the child, is primarily a language, a form of expression, rather than a means of creating beauty.

3. In the beginning the child draws what he knows, rather than what he sees (Verworn's " ideoplastic stage "). Later on he reaches a stage in which he attempts to draw objects as he sees them. The transition from the first stage to the second one is a gradual and continuous process.

4. The ideoplastic basis of children's drawings is shown most conspicuously in the relative proportions given to the separate parts. The child exaggerates the size of items which seem interesting or important; other parts are minimized or omitted.

5. The order of development in drawing is remarkably constant, even among children of very different social antecedents. The reports of investigators the world over show very close agreement, both as regards the method of indicating the separate items in a drawing and the order in which these items tend to appear. This is especially true as regards the human figure, probably because of its universal familiarity.

6. The earliest drawings made by children consist almost entirely of what may be described as a graphic enumeration of items. Ideas of number, of the relative proportion of parts, and of spatial relationships are much later in developing.

7. In drawing objects placed before them young children pay little or no attention to the model. Their drawings from the object are not likely to differ in any important respect from their memory drawings.

8. Drawings made by subnormal children resemble those of younger normal children in their lack of detail and in their defective sense of proportion. They often show qualitative differences, however, especially as regards the relationship of the separate parts to each other. Not infrequently the same drawing will be found to combine very primitive with rather mature characteristics.

9. Children of inferior mental ability sometimes copy well, but they rarely do good original work in drawing. Conversely, the child who shows real creative ability in art is likely to rank high in general mental ability.

10. There is much disagreement among investigators regarding the relationship between children's drawings and those made by primitive or prehistoric races. Until more careful study has been made of the many factors involved in such comparison, the legitimacy of drawing conclusions appears to be very doubtful.

11. Marked sex differences, usually in favor of the boys, are reported by several investigators, especially by Kerschensteiner and Ivanoff.

12. Up to about the age of ten years children draw the human figure in preference to any other subject.

CHAPTER TWO

Experimental Basis of the Drawing Test of Intelligence

METHOD OF APPROACH

THE studies which were described in the preceding chapter appear to show rather clearly that the nature and content of children's drawings are dependent primarily upon intellectual development. Previous attempts to classify these drawings have, however, been very crude. The classifications usually included only a very small number of categories, to one or another of which a drawing was assigned by simple inspection, without formal analysis. The categories were defined in very general terms, thus allowing considerable opportunity for subjective factors to play a part in the classification. It is obvious that while distinctions might be made between groups, individual ratings obtained by such a method could have but little significance.

In the derivation of the scale used in the present experiment the method of approach differed from that of previous investigators in the following respects:

1. No arbitrary decisions have been made as to what does or does not constitute intellectual merit in a drawing.

2. Artistic standards have been entirely disregarded.

3. Every effort has been made to eliminate the subjective element in judgments. Each characteristic dealt with has been defined in as objective terms as possible.

4. A double criterion for judging mental development — chronological age and school grade — was decided upon as a basis for determining the validity of the test and for establishing norms. Supplementary criteria were also used whenever available.

5. A standard subject for drawing was chosen in the begin-

ning and adhered to throughout; but in order to allow as much freedom as possible in the working out of the task, no further specifications were made as to how the drawing should be done.

In the outset of the experiment it was hoped that it would be possible to allow each child to choose his own subject for drawing. Such a method would have the unquestionable advantage of affording a better index to the nature of individual interests than does the one employed. It soon became evident, however, that the plan was not feasible, since, without a careful and systematic study of the relative difficulty of the various subjects which might be chosen, it would be quite impossible to decide with certainty whether a greater degree of ability (of any sort) is shown by a good representation of an easy subject or by a poor representation of a subject which is more difficult. An additional complication is introduced by the fact that, as Maitland (74), Ballard (5, 6), and Katzaroff (56) have shown, the older and brighter children who tend to be more critical of their work are more likely to select the "easier" subjects for drawing.

In deciding upon a subject, the following considerations were held to be of paramount importance:

1. It must be something with which all children are equally familiar. That is, either the situation presented must be an entirely new one, or else all the subjects must have had as nearly as possible equal opportunity to become familiar with it. For very little children, at least, the latter circumstance is probably the more favorable, since it is less likely to produce mental confusion and has the additional advantage of measuring the learning factor as shown by present accomplishment.

2. It must present as little variability in its essential characteristics as possible.

3. It must be simple in its general outline, so that even very little children will be able to attempt it, yet sufficiently complicated in its detail to tax the abilities of an adult.

4. In order that a proper spirit may be maintained among the children taking the test, the subject chosen must be one of universal interest and appeal.

The one subject which seems to fulfill all these requirements to a major degree is the human figure. After some consideration it was decided that the greater uniformity of men's clothing made "a man" a more suitable object for the test than "a woman" or "a child." "A man," therefore, was the subject finally chosen.

SUBJECTS

In the fall of 1920, through the kindness of Miss Alice Mehleis, at that time supervisor of primary grades in Perth Amboy, New Jersey, and with the coöperation of the teachers under her direction, nearly 4000 drawings were obtained from children in the kindergartens and first four grades of the public schools of that city. These drawings were made under standardized conditions essentially the same as those described in Part II. From these, a group of one hundred drawings was selected for preliminary study. The basis of selection was age-grade classification, as shown below:

AGE	GRADE	NO. OF DRAWINGS
4-0 to 4-11	Kindergarten	10
5-0 to 5-11	Kindergarten	10
6-0 to 6-5	Low first	10
6-6 to 6-11	High first	10
7-0 to 7-5	Low second	10
7-6 to 7-11	High second	10
8-0 to 8-5	Low third	10
8-6 to 8-11	High third	10
9-0 to 9-5	Low fourth	10
9-6 to 9-11	High fourth	10

The selection was a random one as far as all other factors are concerned.

These drawings were then spread out in order, and careful observations were made to determine in what respects the drawings in the upper groups appeared to differ from those in the lower groups; that is, to determine what characteristic changes take place in children's drawings with increasing age and intellectual development. No *a priori* assumptions were made as to the probable nature of these changes, and the artistic effect of the differences which were observed was entirely disregarded. The only point considered was that of comparative differences.

Several persons in addition to the writer were asked to study the drawings from this standpoint. The characteristics noted were defined as objectively as possible, and on the basis of these pooled observations a rough scale of about forty separate "points"[1] was devised. This first crude scale will not be described in detail. It was based chiefly upon presence or absence of various parts of the body, and the relationship of these parts to each other.

The one hundred drawings which had been selected were then scored according to this plan. Each point was recorded separately, and curves were plotted, showing the comparative number of successes at each age level.

VALIDATION OF THE SEPARATE POINTS

A threefold criterion was used for determining the validity of each point. The requirements were: (1) a regular and (2) fairly rapid increase in the percentage of children suc-

---

[1] A "point" is defined as a single unit of the scale. It may be based upon the presence or absence of a specified element, upon the method of representation of a given quantitative or spatial relationship, upon eye-hand coördination, or several of these characteristics may have been combined to form a single "point."

ceeding with the point at successive ages, and (3) a clear differentiation between the performances of children who were of the same age but in different school grades.[1] It was also required that the rules for scoring be objectively defined in terms which were broad enough to cover all situations that were likely to arise.

Even from the small number of cases used, it was evident that the scoring of many of the points would have to be changed. The scale was therefore revised, other points which had suggested themselves were added, and the drawings were then re-scored according to the new plan. The resulting curves were reasonably satisfactory, as far as the group under consideration was concerned. All the drawings from one school building, about 800 in number, were then scored, the results were tabulated, and curves were plotted as before. On the basis of these findings the scale was again revised and extended.

In all, five revisions of the scale have been made, the same general procedure being followed in each case. A different set of drawings was used for each revision in order to avoid the error of validating a point by means of the same drawings from which it had been derived. The scale in its present form consists of 51 points, each one of which has been shown to conform fairly well to the requirements laid down. (See page 17.)

It is unnecessary to present the four preliminary scales. Many of the points were essentially the same as those in the final form of the scale, though there are few instances in which the actual method of scoring has not undergone some modification. This is particularly true of the several points having to do with the method of representing clothing and

[1] The third criterion could not be used in this preliminary analysis, since the cases had been selected on an age-grade basis. It was used in all subsequent validation.

with sense of proportion. Point 12 *a* is an example. The various methods tried for scoring this point were as follows:

SCALE 1. Head smaller than trunk.

Objection: Too crude a measure. The curve showed only a slight increase in the percentage of successes at different ages.

SCALE 2. Head length not less than one tenth or greater than one fifth of the total body length.

Objection: In many instances there appears to be a negative correlation between the size of the head and the length of the legs. Sometimes this fact is determined by the size of the sheet of paper — the child who makes a very large head and trunk being obliged to make the legs very short in order to get them on the page. Conversely, the child who makes a small head and trunk may thriftily fill up the remaining space with a pair of abnormally drawn-out legs. To compare the several parts with the total often has the effect of penalizing the child twice for a single disproportionate element.

SCALE 3. Size of head " not grossly disproportionate to the remainder of the drawing."

Objection: Too indefinite a ruling, leading to subjective errors in scoring. The method was tried largely to see whether the point was worth using at all, as both previous methods had resulted in very unsatisfactory curves. The results obtained in this way showed clearly that the point was one which should be retained in the scale; accordingly another method of scoring was tried.

SCALE 4. Both vertical and horizontal measurements of head less than the corresponding measurements of the trunk.

Objection: This method applies very well to full-face drawings, but it is not satisfactory with profiles.

SCALE 5. Area of head not more than one half or less than one tenth that of the trunk.

This is the method finally adopted.

It will be seen that the general procedure employed has been of the " cut and try " sort. A point which appeared to have differentiating value was noted, and a method of scoring was then devised. If the results showed a clear separation of different age and grade groups, the point was retained; if not, other scoring methods were tried. When no satisfactory scoring method could be found, the point was rejected. Typical examples of rejected points are the following:

1. *Teeth shown.*

Up to about the age of seven, the curve shows a regular increase in the percentage of children who draw the teeth. After this age there is an equally marked decrease, a fact which renders the point useless.

2. *Attempt to show color by shading.*

This varies according to the hardness of the lead and the condition of the point of the pencil used.

3. *Attempt to represent movement, as walking or running.*

This point was rejected only after several attempts to score it had been made. There is little doubt as to its being, in some degree, a valid indication of intellectual maturity. The difficulty lies in differentiating between real attempts to show movement and mere bad coördination. As a result of poor coördination the drawing may seem to show one leg being raised, as in walking, when nothing of the sort was intended by the child. With the more mature drawings it is usually possible to make the distinction, but with those of the younger children it is often difficult, if not impossible, to do so.

4. *Pupils of eyes symmetrically placed, so as to focus the glance correctly.*

Gives too much weight to eye details, and is difficult to score consistently. A modification of the point has been retained (16 *d*).

5. *Entire figure in correct alignment. If the full-face position has been chosen, all parts must be in full face. If the profile has been shown, all parts must face in the same direction.*

The curve shows a very marked drop from eight to ten years, due to the confusion which arises at the time of transition from the full-face to the profile drawing.

Other points were rejected for reasons analogous to those just cited. It is probable that in some instances further trials might disclose methods of scoring which would do away with the objections mentioned, but such methods have not yet been found.

A list of the fifty-one points included in the present form of the scale follows. Directions for scoring are given in Part II.

Outline of the Scale

Class A

Preliminary stage, in which the drawing cannot be recognized as the human figure.

1. Aimless, uncontrolled scribbling.
2. Lines somewhat controlled, approaching crude geometrical forms.

Class B

Drawings which can be recognized as the human figure. The fifty-one points have reference to drawings of this class.

1. Head present.
2. Legs present.

3.   Arms present.
4 *a*. Trunk present.
4 *b*. Length of trunk greater than breadth.
4 *c*. Shoulders indicated.
5 *a*. Both arms and legs attached to trunk.
5 *b*. Legs attached to trunk. Arms attached to trunk at the correct point.
6 *a*. Neck present.
6 *b*. Outline of neck continuous with that of head, of trunk, or of both.
7 *a*. Eyes present.
7 *b*. Nose present.
7 *c*. Mouth present.
7 *d*. Both nose and mouth shown in two dimensions; two lips shown.
7 *e*. Nostrils indicated.
8 *a*. Hair shown.
8 *b*. Hair present on more than the circumference of the head, and non-transparent. Method of representation better than a scribble.
9 *a*. Clothing present.
9 *b*. Two articles of clothing non-transparent.
9 *c*. Entire drawing free from transparencies when both sleeves and trousers are shown.
9 *d*. Four or more articles of clothing definitely indicated.
9 *e*. Costume complete, without incongruities.
10 *a*. Fingers shown.
10 *b*. Correct number of fingers shown.
10 *c*. Fingers shown in two dimensions, length greater than breadth, and the angle subtended by them not greater than 180 degrees.
10 *d*. Opposition of thumb shown.
10 *e*. Hand shown, as distinct from fingers or arms.

11 *a*. Arm joint shown, — either elbow, shoulder, or both.

11 *b*. Leg joint shown, — either knee, hip, or both.

12 *a*. Head in proportion.

12 *b*. Arms in proportion.

12 *c*. Legs in proportion.

12 *d*. Feet in proportion.

12 *e*. Both arms and legs shown in two dimensions.

13.   Heel shown.

14 *a*. Motor coördination. Lines A (see directions for scoring).

14 *b*. Motor coördination. Lines B.

14 *c*. Motor coördination. Head outline.

14 *d*. Motor coördination. Trunk outline.

14 *e*. Motor coördination. Outline of arms and legs.

14 *f*. Motor coördination. Features.

15 *a*. Ears present.

15 *b*. Ears present in correct position and proportion.

16 *a*. Eye detail. Brow or lashes shown.

16 *b*. Eye detail. Pupil shown.

16 *c*. Eye detail. Proportion.

16 *d*. Eye detail. Glance directed to front in profile drawings.

17 *a*. Both chin and forehead shown.

17 *b*. Projection of chin shown.

18 *a*. Profile with not more than one error.

18 *b*. Correct profile.

In Table 1 the percentages succeeding with each of the separate points have been summarized according to age and school progress. The figures are based upon the 3593 cases used in the original standardization of the test. The composition of this group is described in the following section. These facts are shown graphically in Plates I–IX.

TABLE 1

PER CENT SUCCEEDING WITH EACH OF THE SEPARATE POINTS IN THE SCALE BY AGE AND SCHOOL PROGRESS.¹ ORIGINAL GROUP

Age	4	5		6		7			8			9			10	
Key No.	N	A	N	A	N	A	N	R	A	N	R	A	N	R	N	R
1	94	100	99	100	100	100	100	93	100	100	100	100	100	100	100	100
2	85	100	96	100	99	100	100	96	100	100	100	100	100	100	100	100
3	55	80	64	87	83	96	88	80	92	91	81	100	92	91	98	90
4 a	59	100	74	100	87	100	99	92	100	99	98	100	100	98	100	100
4 b	10	20	22	49	33	55	48	42	65	49	51	88	62	57	75	53
4 c	0	0	1	6	2	13	7	2	29	12	7	52	25	10	46	19
5 a	21	70	44	82	66	93	85	73	93	87	79	100	92	89	97	89
5 b	2	30	9	17	12	33	24	14	54	33	23	72	47	28	59	38
6 a	5	40	14	32	26	61	44	26	80	66	39	88	74	57	83	59
6 b	0	0	1	16	6	17	16	7	49	32	17	72	45	24	65	36
7 a	81	100	93	100	98	100	98	96	100	98	98	100	99	98	100	99
7 b	54	100	78	93	90	100	95	93	100	97	96	100	100	97	100	98
7 c	58	90	80	96	90	96	91	91	97	92	90	100	94	91	96	90
7 d	0	0	0	9	2	18	18	0	43	24	7	55	35	30	73	44
7 e	2	0	4	15	3	19	8	5	22	13	3	56	22	10	27	15
8 a	16	0	13	22	16	46	22	21	46	45	25	64	45	35	58	41
8 b	0	0	0	1	0	5	5	0	17	10	5	52	17	5	35	13
9 a	27	90	35	91	75	99	94	78	99	98	92	100	98	98	100	90
9 b	0	20	0	2	2	17	8	2	38	19	9	64	42	19	58	26
9 c	0	0	0	0	0	1	1	0	6	3	0	36	7	0	24	3
9 d	0	0	0	2	0	5	3	0	31	11	6	68	26	10	49	18
9 e	0	0	0	0	0	0	0	0	2	0	0	20	5	0	15	3
10 a	32	60	49	83	69	90	77	72	90	78	75	95	86	79	93	78
10 b	4	10	10	37	19	47	35	16	49	41	29	50	45	36	57	37

10 c	0	0	3	17	7	19	14	6	22	19	13	44	26	16	41	25
10 d	0	0	0	1	1	3	1	0	6	3	0	12	5	2	13	3
10 e	6	20	5	14	12	26	14	6	40	29	12	60	36	22	48	28
11 a	1	10	2	6	5	30	18	5	48	26	14	68	48	26	64	30
11 b	1	20	3	13	8	22	13	7	45	31	17	64	40	26	53	32
12 a	20	40	33	49	38	66	53	87	70	69	49	80	72	63	76	58
12 b	1	20	8	16	13	42	23	14	35	30	22	45	44	29	47	34
12 c	8	50	29	52	39	57	50	38	68	62	49	67	62	52	64	53
12 d	12	70	27	42	42	59	60	49	74	64	55	80	67	65	76	74
12 e	9	60	27	66	50	87	66	51	95	86	68	100	92	84	98	80
13	1	20	4	10	10	36	18	10	45	37	19	64	52	37	66	38
14 a	2	40	18	50	35	70	54	47	91	77	61	100	88	74	93	76
14 b	0	0	0	0	0	0	0	0	3	0	0	8	2	0	9	1
14 c	0	0	0	2	1	9	5	3	25	17	6	56	33	12	44	27
14 d	0	0	0	9	2	16	8	3	46	17	7	48	35	14	48	28
14 e	0	0	1	1	1	1	2	1	17	3	2	20	14	5	23	16
14 f	0	0	0	0	0	0	0	0	2	2	1	56	4	1	23	5
15 a	0	10	0	22	24	39	27	24	40	32	28	40	35	29	36	32
15 b	1	0	1	4	2	13	9	4	31	14	7	36	14	12	28	15
16 a	2	20	9	43	26	57	42	26	63	55	37	72	58	52	68	56
16 b	3	10	7	15	9	24	15	6	40	21	12	80	35	20	37	27
16 c	0	0	1	6	4	8	9	4	25	16	6	60	26	10	33	18
16 d	0	0	0	2	0	2	1	0	3	1	0	12	4	0	7	2
17 a	7	20	18	43	39	54	56	41	74	66	57	90	84	66	90	78
17 b	0	0	0	2	0	7	5	1	18	15	10	30	24	12	31	19
18 a	0	0	0	0	1	12	2	1	14	7	4	28	20	4	28	11
18 b	0	0	0	0	0	1	0	0	1	1	0	12	3	0	10	3

¹ See page 36.

A = Children accelerated in school.   N = Children who have made normal school progress.

R = Children retarded in school. The limits of these groups and the number of cases are shown in Table 2.

PLATE I

PER CENT SUCCEEDING WITH POINTS 1 TO 4c BY AGE AND SCHOOL
PROGRESS

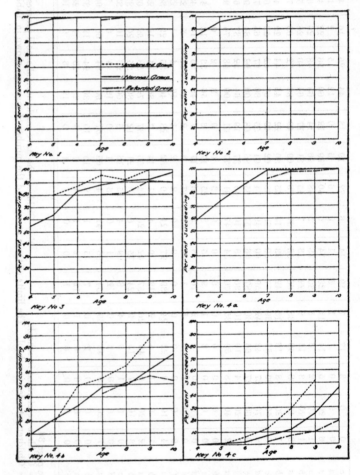

PLATE II

PER CENT SUCCEEDING WITH POINTS 5 *a* TO 7 *b* BY AGE AND SCHOOL PROGRESS

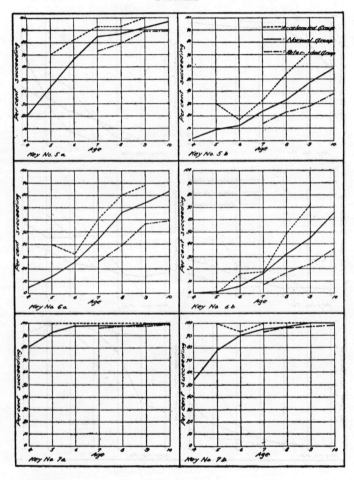

PLATE III

PER CENT SUCCEEDING WITH POINTS 7 c TO 9 a BY AGE AND SCHOOL PROGRESS

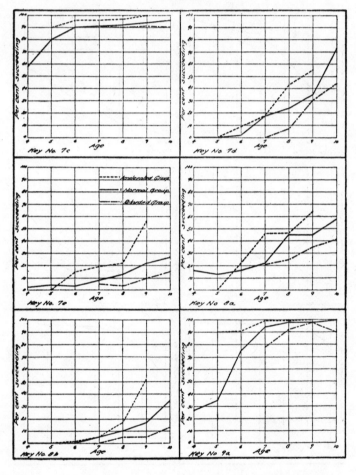

PLATE IV

PER CENT SUCCEEDING WITH POINTS 9 *b* TO 10 *b* BY AGE AND SCHOOL PROGRESS

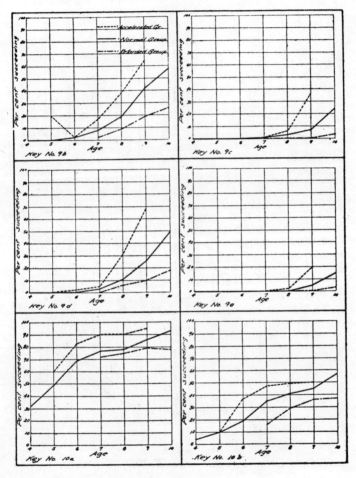

PLATE V

PER CENT SUCCEEDING WITH POINTS 10 *c* TO 12 *a* BY AGE AND SCHOOL
PROGRESS

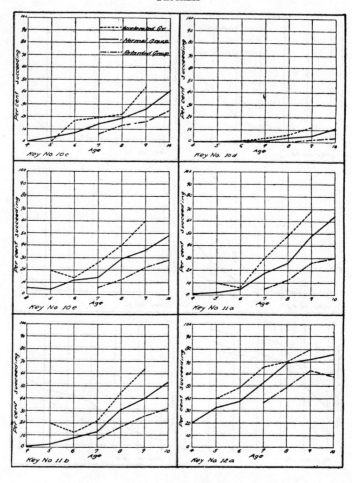

PLATE VI

PER CENT SUCCEEDING WITH POINTS 12 *b* TO 14 *a* BY AGE AND SCHOOL
PROGRESS

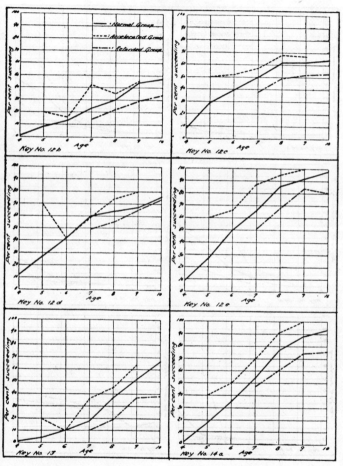

PLATE VII

PER CENT SUCCEEDING WITH POINTS 14 b TO 15 a BY AGE AND SCHOOL PROGRESS

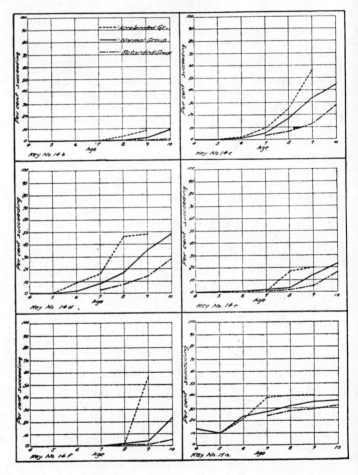

PLATE VIII

PER CENT SUCCEEDING WITH POINTS 15 *b* TO 17 *a* BY AGE AND SCHOOL
PROGRESS

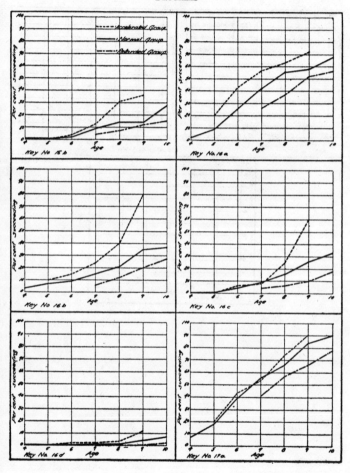

PLATE IX

Per Cent Succeeding with Points 17 *b* to 18 *b* by Age and School Progress

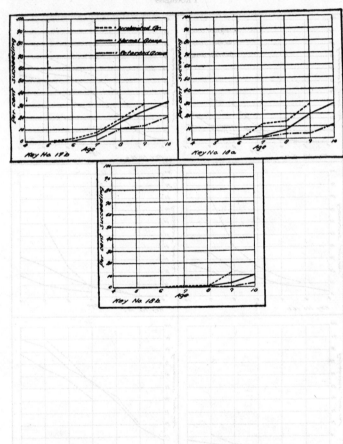

For comparison with the data presented in Table 1, the following figures, which are taken from Partridge's (*89*) report of the drawings made by English children a quarter of a century ago, are of interest. Partridge's figures are based on 200 cases at each age.

PER CENT OF CHILDREN SHOWING DIFFERENT PARTS OF THE BODY AT SUCCESSIVE AGE LEVELS

Age	4	5	6	7	8	9	10
Hair:							
Partridge	6	26	27	32	38	58	70
Goodenough normal group .	16	13	16	22	45	45	58
Neck:							
Partridge	8	22	20	37	51	63	79
Goodenough normal group .	5	14	26	44	66	74	83
Arms:							
Partridge	45	67	71	80	76	85	93
Goodenough normal group .	55	64	83	88	91	92	98
Trunk:							
Partridge	50	82	92	93	98	99	98
Goodenough normal group .	59	74	87	99	99	100	100

Considering the small number of cases and the possible differences in method of scoring, the agreement between the findings is significant. The order of appearance of the four items is the same in both cases : the trunk first, then the arms, neck, and hair. The large number of four-year-olds in the normal group who show the hair is probably a fluctuation due to sampling, as the number of cases — 119 — at that age is relatively small.

DERIVATION OF AGE NORMS

Drawings from 3593 children, ranging in age from 4 to 10 years, were used in the final standardization of the scale. These drawings were obtained from the following schools :

Perth Amboy, New Jersey. Six schools, kindergarten to fourth grade, together with two fifth-grade classes. Ages 4–10 were included. Number of drawings, 2995.

South Orange, New Jersey. Seven classes, Grades 1–5. Ages 5–10 were included. Number of drawings, 247.

East Orange, New Jersey. Grades 1–2. Number of drawings, 86.

Bogota, New Jersey. Five classes, Grades 2–5. Ages 6–10 were included. Number of drawings, 167.

Private school, New York City. Ages 4–10, regardless of grade, were included. Number of drawings, 44.

Miscellaneous small groups, ages 4–10. Number of drawings, 54.

The last five groups, totaling 598 cases, are made up for the most part of children of American parentage and of rather better than average social status. The Perth Amboy group contains a disproportionately large number of children of South European descent — this in spite of the fact that the drawings from two schools in which the population was almost exclusively foreign or negro were not included in these distributions. Racial origin was, unfortunately, not ascertained at the time these drawings were secured, hence precise figures are not available. However, data obtained afterward from the schools indicate that not more than 25 per cent of the 2995 children were of American-born white parentage. The range of nationalities is extensive, but Italians, Slavs, Greeks, German and Russian Jews, Poles, Hungarians, Danes, and negroes predominate.

Scores were tabulated according to age and school grade. In the final summarizing these groups were combined into three main classes at each age, designated as A, N, and R. Under A were included those children who were accelerated in school, under N those who were in a grade corresponding roughly to their chronological age, and under R those who were retarded. The standards used in making this classification are given at the end of Table 2. A certain amount of overlapping between the N and the R groups has been allowed because of varying age of school entrance, but the standards are somewhat more strict than those used by Ayres (250). The assumption made here is that the majority of children enter first grade between the ages of six and six and one half years. It is, of course, true that some children do not enter until seven, but in the schools under consideration this number is more than counterbalanced by those who enter before six. Since ages were taken as at mid-term, no child would be classed as retarded unless he had failed of promotion at least once, or had not entered school until after the age of six years and nine months. Children who enter before the age of six years and three months might make from one to three failures (according to the age of entrance) before being classed as retarded, while those who enter before the age of five years and nine months and make regular progress thereafter would be classed as accelerated after one or two promotions. It is obviously impossible to formulate any general scheme which will allow either for all individual cases within a single locality or for variations in school curricula and promotion standards in different localities.

In spite of the elimination of the two foreign schools and the addition of 598 cases from a more favorable environment and better social class, Table 2 shows that the proportion of retarded children is still very great. Comparison of the grade status of the children from the different localities showed that Perth Amboy was furnishing far more than her normal quota of these retarded children. The fact is especially noteworthy, as this was the only school system in the group in which the generality of school children were sent

TABLE 2

DISTRIBUTION OF TOTAL SCORES BY AGE AND SCHOOL PROGRESS.[1] ORIGINAL GROUP

SCORE	4	5		6		7			8			9			10	
	N	A	N	A	N	A	N	R	A	N	R	A	N	R	N	R
0–2	13		6		3			2								
3–5	39		36		12			2			1					
6–8	37		111		62		1	13			5			2		
9–11	22	1	111	10	90	1	5	58		3	23			9		4
12–14	7	5	63	20	127	5	81	62		23	49		17	22		21
15–17	1	2	35	25	144	13	153	45	6	35	85		28	54	5	42
18–20		1	13	11	63	17	122	9	8	58	59		41	63	9	64
21–23		1		7	9	20	45	3	16	77	13		43	98	14	56
24–26				6	5	11	23	1	11	50	10	2	55	25	27	56
27–29				2		6	18		8	33	2	2	42	15	36	30
30–32				1		2	8		7	10	1	5	45	2	38	12
33–35						1	1		6	4		4	29		32	6
36–38									1	3		3	14		22	3
39–41									2	2		4	11		21	1
42–44												2	4		4	1
45–47												1			3	
48–50												2			2	
Total cases	119	10	375	82	515	76	457	195	65	298	248	25	329	290	213	296
Mdn.	6.1	13.9	9.4	15.8	13.6	20.8	17.3	12.6	24.2	21.7	16.1	32.1	25.4	20.3	30.7	21.4
Mean	6.3	14.8	9.8	16.6	13.3	20.9	18.0	12.7	25.2	21.8	16.2	32.9	25.7	19.7	30.8	21.8
S.D.	3.3	3.3	3.9	4.8	4.3	4.7	4.3	3.6	6.0	5.3	4.1	6.7	7.1	4.3	6.7	5.6
LIMITS OF GROUPS																
Upper limit	Kg	H1	L1	L2	H1	L3	H2	L1	L4	H3	L2	L5	H4	L3	H5	L4
Lower limit	Kg	H1	Kg	L2	Kg	L3	H1	L1	L4	H2	L2	L5	H3	L3	H4	L4

[1] A = Accelerated group.   N = Normal group.   R = Retarded group.

into first grade at the age of five. It will also be remembered that the great majority of these children were of South European descent.

The great amount of retardation led to the belief that norms based upon the total number of children without regard to grade location would be too low. It was therefore decided to disregard both the A and the R groups, and standardize upon the basis of the N distribution alone. In this group the means for the successive ages, taken to the nearest whole number, are as follows:

Age	Mean
4	6
5	10
6	13
7	18
8	22
9	25
10	31

Smoothing the curve and extrapolating at both extremes give the following as tentative age norms:

Age	Norm
3	2
4	6
5	10
6	14
7	18
8	22
9	26
10	30
11	34
12	38
13	42

Ages were taken to the last birthday; hence the above norms apply to the interval midway between birthdays, as $6\frac{1}{2}$ years, etc.

By substituting the age norms as given in the table for the point score earned on the drawing, the approximate mental age of a child may be found. The intelligence quotient (or IQ) is then obtained by dividing the mental age by the chronological age. Chronological ages above 13 years are considered as 13 only in calculating the IQ, since the scale does not measure mental ages above 13.

In order to check the above norms, drawings were secured from three other localities and the scores tabulated in the same manner. Means and standard deviations are shown separately in Tables 3, 4, and 5. It will be seen that the means for the A, N, and R groups do not vary greatly from those found previously, but that the separate localities differ very markedly in the proportion of children found within each of these groups. The Rutherford cases (Table 3) include all children between the ages of six and twelve years who were enrolled in the first five grades of the public schools of that city in December, 1920. Practically all are of American parentage. Other tests given there at the same time indicate that the median IQ is not far from 107. The age-grade distribution of the Fresno children (Table 4), all of whom are taken from the first six grades of a single school, also suggests a superior intellectual average, while for the Southern whites (Table 5) the reverse situation is found. The scores made on the drawing scale are roughly proportional to the amount of school retardation and suggest a true difference in the average mental capacity of the several groups.

Table 6 (on page 43) shows the distribution of scores made by 363 children from thirteen kindergartens of Santa Clara County, California. The combined results from the five groups by age and school progress are shown in Table 7. The data of Table 7 are shown graphically in Plate X (on page 45).

TABLE 3

Means and Standard Deviations of Total Scores by Age and School Progress.[1] Rutherford Group

Age	6 A	6 N	7 A	7 N	7 R	8 A	8 N	8 R	9 A	9 N	9 R	10 N	10 R	11 N	11 R	12 R
Total cases	13	100	15	80	14	16	92	21	17	83	24	73	22	38	18	26
Mean	20.8	15.5	23.8	19.8	16.9	29.3	24.0	18.0	30.1	28.0	21.9	31.1	28.4	30.7	26.0	28.7
S.D.	4.9	4.2	4.9	4.3	5.8	4.1	4.4	5.7	5.6	6.4	5.9	6.3	7.0	6.2	7.4	6.4

For limits of groups see Table 4.

TABLE 4

Means and Standard Deviations of Total Scores by Age and School Progress. Fresno Group

Age	6 A	6 N	7 A	7 N	7 R	8 A	8 N	8 R	9 A	9 N	9 R	10 A	10 N	10 R	11 N	11 R	12 N	12 R
Total cases	14	93	15	45	9	12	56	2	16	43	7	22	30	14	63	7	22	9
Mean	19.6	15.5	20.8	20.1	16.3	26.7	24.1	20.5	30.8	27.9	27.1	33.9	29.7	30.4	34.3	26.3	35.2	28.0
S.D.	3.8	4.5	4.5	5.4	3.6	6.9	5.4	4.5	6.1	6.4	6.4	7.2	6.2	6.0	6.5	7.1	6.2	4.9

[1] A = Accelerated group.   N = Normal group.   R = Retarded group.

TABLE 5

MEANS AND STANDARD DEVIATIONS OF TOTAL SCORES BY AGE AND SCHOOL PROGRESS.[1] SOUTHERN WHITES

Age	6		7			8			9		10		11	12
	A	N	A	N	R	A	N	R	N	R	N	R	R	R
Total cases . . .	7	42	3	87	25	4	57	40	49	62	35	53	48	28
Mean	24.6	15.3	20.0	19.0	16.8	18.3	22.6	16.8	25.4	20.8	28.7	23.4	24.2	24.1
S. D.	5.4	4.2	3.7	5.8	4.4	4.4	6.2	5.9	7.1	6.9	7.2	6.5	6.7	5.1

For limits of groups, see Table 4.
Grades I-IV are included in this table.

[1] A = Accelerated group. N = Normal group. R = Retarded group.

TABLE 6

DISTRIBUTION OF TOTAL SCORES. SANTA CLARA COUNTY KINDERGARTENS

AGE	4	5	6	7	8
SCORE					
0–2	1	2			
3–5	19	23		1	
6–8	13	56	11	2	1
9–11	12	61	13	2	
12–14	8	52	15		
15–17	4	43	6		
18–20		8	5		
21–23		3	1		
24–26			0		
27–29			1		
Total cases	57	248	52	5	1
Mdn.	7.5	10.6	11.9	7.75	7.0
Mean	8.0	10.8	12.4	7.6	7.0
S. D.	3.9	4.2	4.5		

The data presented in Tables 3–7 indicate that the tentative norms given on page 39 may be slightly too easy at the lower end of the scale, and too difficult at the upper end. That the error, if it exists, is not great is shown by the distribution of IQ's which have been calculated on this basis for the Rutherford, Fresno, and Southern white groups (Table 8). The character of the population, which includes two superior groups and one which is slightly inferior, leads to the expectation of a mean IQ slightly above 100. This is found to be the case if we take the average for the boys and girls at each age up to nine years, after which age we no longer have a representative group, since the brightest children have been promoted to grades not included in the survey. The unusually high average of the six-year-olds can be accounted for by the fact that kindergarten children were

TABLE 7

Distribution of Total Scores by Age and School Progress.[1] Total Cases

Age	4	5	5	6	6	7	7	7	8	8	8	9	9	9	10	10	10	11	11	12	12
Score	N	A	N	A	N	A	N	R	A	N	R	A	N	R	A	N	R	N	R	N	R
0–2	14	1	8		3																
3–5	58	5	59		13		2	2													
6–8	50	2	167	10	76	1	11	3		4	2										
9–11	34	1	172	20	140	7	107	15	1	29	8		20	2		1					
12–14	15	1	115	34	208	18	199	63	7	52	29	1	35	12		7					
15–17	5		78	21	209	21	173	77	12	85	59	1	57	32	1	16	5		2		1
18–20			21	13	109	29	88	59	19	134	102	3	78	70		27	22	9	5		1
21–23			3	11	30	19	40	17	17	97	70	6	80	84	3	49	51	12	17		7
24–26				3	9	9	30	6	13	52	20	11	64	107	3	52	70	12	4	2	14
27–29				2	3	3	13	3	12	28	15	15	69	38	3	60	79	14	9	3	11
30–32				2	2	3	6	2	12	14	2	5	52	19	3	56	72	18	7	3	9
33–35						2		1	1	5	5	9	24	13	1	36	38	10	10	2	9
36–38									2	3		3	19	3	4	35	22	16	3	5	5
39–41									1			1	6	2	3	7	9	8	1	4	4
42–44												3		1	1	3	6	1	4	2	2
45–47																2	1	1	0	0	
48–50																	1		1	1	
Total cases	176	10	623	116	802	109	669	248	97	503	312	58	504	383	22	351	385	101	73	22	63
Mdn.	6.5	13.9	9.9	17.5	13.9	21.3	17.8	13.1	25.2	22.3	16.2	30.9	25.8	20.2	33.5	30.7	22.2	33.1	23.2	36.1	25.8
Mean	6.9	14.8	10.2	17.9	13.9	21.2	18.5	13.4	25.8	22.5	16.4	31.5	26.2	20.2	33.9	30.6	22.7	33.0	24.8	35.2	26.6
S. D.	3.6	3.3	4.1	5.3	4.4	4.8	4.7	4.2	6.2	5.4	4.5	6.4	7.0	5.1	7.2	6.6	6.2	6.6	7.0	6.2	6.0

[1] A = Accelerated group.   N = Normal group.   R = Retarded group.

44

PLATE X

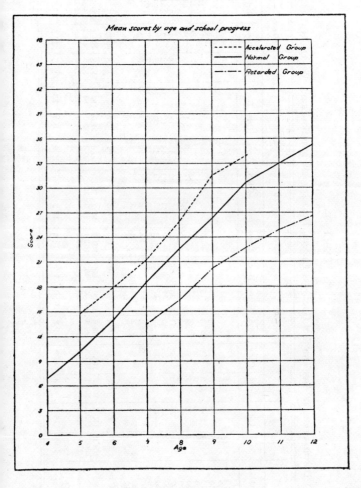

TABLE 8

IQ Distribution by Age and Sex Groups. Fresno, Rutherford, and Southern Whites (Combined)

AGE / IQ	6 Boys	6 Girls	7 Boys	7 Girls	8 Boys	8 Girls	9 Boys	9 Girls	10 Boys	10 Girls	11 Boys	11 Girls	12 Boys	12 Girls	Totals Boys	Totals Girls	Total Both Sexes
170	1		1												2	0	2
160	1	1	0												1	1	2
150	0	3	0	4	1										1	7	8
140	4	1	2	6	3	2	3	1							12	10	22
130	9	9	9	6	8	7	8	10	2						36	32	68
120	13	22	11	17	8	21	13	19	20	17	3	1			68	97	165
110	22	33	32	23	23	23	20	21	10	16	15	11			122	127	249
100	34	29	39	32	31	36	33	23	20	32	13	18	7	5	177	175	352
90	30	21	28	30	33	31	30	33	25	20	14	17	14	2	174	154	328
80	18	13	25	14	25	17	28	11	35	13	13	20	16	8	160	96	256
70	4	1	7	4	14	7	16	17	18	10	18	16	10	7	87	62	149
60			1	2	6	1	9	4	6	3	9	3	9	6	40	19	59
50					2	1	1	1	2		2	1	1		8	3	11
40																	
Total Cases	136	133	155	138	154	146	161	140	138	111	87	87	57	28	888	783	1671
Mdn.	104.2	110.3	103.7	105.4	98.6	103.9	98.3	101.2	92.7	102.5	90.6	91.6	84.8	80.8	98.1	102.8	100.4
Mean	106.4	110.4	104.1	107.5	99.4	104.4	98.7	102.1	95.3	101.1	90.8	92.0	84.0	82.0	98.7	102.9	100.7
S.D.	17.9	16.5	17.0	18.7	19.1	16.6	19.2	19.2	18.3	15.9	18.1	14.9	13.0	13.5	19.0	18.3	18.8
Coef. of var.	16.8	14.9	16.3	17.4	19.2	15.9	19.5	18.8	19.2	15.7	19.9	16.2	15.5	16.5	19.3	17.8	18.7

not included, and also by the fact that, as will be seen by referring to Table 5, the proportion of Southern whites is much smaller at this age than at any other.   Upon the whole it has not seemed advisable to make any change in the original standards upon the basis of the data thus far obtained, although it is possible that later findings may lead to some adjustment along the lines indicated.

CHAPTER THREE

DISCUSSION OF RESULTS

RELIABILITY

DATA on the statistical evaluation of the test and its results have been presented elsewhere[1] and will not be repeated in detail. It has been found that the correlation between original scores and scores earned by a retest on the following day was .937 $\pm$ .006 for 194 first-grade children. The average reliability computed by the " split scale " method (using the Spearman-Brown formula [2]) was found to be .77 for ages five to ten taken separately. The probable error of estimate of a true IQ earned on the drawing test is approximately 5.4 points at all ages from five to ten years.

Additional evidence as to the reliability of a test is furnished by the variability of the scores within single age groups. In general it may be said that the greater the variability the less reliable is the test. The data from Table 7 (page 44) were therefore combined, and the standard deviations thus obtained were transmuted into terms of mental age months. The results are shown below.

AGE	4	5	6	7	8	9	10
S. D.	10.8	12.3	14.1	15.6	18.6	21.6	22.8
C. V.[3]	.19[4]	.19	.18	.17	.18	.19	.18

[1] Goodenough, Florence L.: "A New Approach to the Measurement of the Intelligence of Young Children." *Pedagogical Seminary and Journal of Genetic Psychology*, Vol. 33 (June, 1926).

[2] $r_{12} = \dfrac{2\,r_{11}}{1 + r_{11}}$.

[3] Coefficient of variability.

[4] The mean age for the four-year-old group was four years and nine months. At all other ages the cases were distributed fairly evenly within the group, thus placing the mean at the half-year interval.

These figures correspond fairly closely to those reported by Willson [1] on the variability of the Stanford-Binet. Willson's data show a standard deviation of 14.8 months of mental age for unselected six-year-old children.

It should be noted that the coefficient of variability remains very nearly constant for each of the seven age groups considered. Ages eleven and twelve have not been included, since the test does not measure the upper levels of ability at those ages.

VALIDITY

By referring to Tables 2–7 it will be seen that children of the same chronological age vary widely in their performance on this test, and that a significant correlation exists between test score and grade placement. A study of the promotions made during a three-semester period by 162 children who had been tested in the first grade shows that the test has distinct value in predicting future school success. No child in this group whose IQ was below 100 made an extra promotion, and every child whose IQ was below 70 failed of promotion at least once during this period.

In order to determine whether the test contributes anything to a prognosis of school success which is not given by the ordinary type of group intelligence test or by a teachers' judgment of intelligence, a group of 286 fourth and fifth grade children were given the Army Alpha, the drawing test, and Form B of the Trabue Completion. Teachers' estimates of intelligence on a scale of five points were also obtained, and a grade-progress ratio was computed for each child by dividing the number of grades which had been skipped or repeated by the child's chronological age. In the zero order of correlations the Army Alpha was found to show the highest correla-

[1] Willson, G. M.: "Standard Deviations of Age Scores and Quotients in Typical Groups." *Journal of Educational Psychology*, Vol. 16 (1925), pages 193–207.

tion with the grade-progress ratio ($r = .691$), while the drawing test, the Trabue Completion test, and the teachers' estimates correlated .581, .593, and .597, respectively, with the grade-progress ratio. When each of the remaining tests was rendered constant by partial correlation treatment, however (third-order partials), it was found that the correlation between the drawing test and the grade-progress ratio was .377, between Alpha and grade-progress .328, between Trabue and grade-progress .372, and between teachers' estimates of intelligence and grade-progress .250. This indicates that the test measures an aspect of mentality which is in some degree distinct from that measured by the Army Alpha or the Trabue Completion, and which is likely to be disregarded by teachers in their estimates of pupil intelligence.

A total of 334 children have been given both the drawing test and the Stanford-Binet. Correlations between drawing score and Binet mental ages were computed by separate age groups. The results have been summarized in Table 9.

TABLE 9

CORRELATION BETWEEN STANFORD-BINET MENTAL AGE AND DRAWING MENTAL AGE

AGE	NUMBER OF CASES	S. D. BINET	S. D. DRAWING	r
4	25	10.3 mo.	11.5 mo.	.863 ± .034
5	94	11.0 mo.	12.3 mo.	.699 ± .035
6	65	17.3 mo.	18.5 mo.	.832 ± .025
7	63	16.4 mo.	19.2 mo.	.716 ± .042
8	27	14.6 mo.	18.3 mo.	.557 ± .092
9	37	20.4 mo.	24.6 mo.	.728 ± .053
10	23	22.9 mo.	24.8 mo.	.849 ± .041

Correlation between drawing IQ and Stanford-Binet IQ was also computed for the 334 cases included in Table 9. The amount of agreement is shown in Table 10.

TABLE 10

CORRELATION BETWEEN STANFORD-BINET IQ AND DRAWING IQ, AGES 4–10

IQ-Binet \ IQ-Drawing	40	50	60	70	80	90	100	110	120	130	140	150	160	170	N
170															
160															
150															
140									1		1			1	3
130					1				4	4	1			1	11
120					2	2	2	3	4	1	2				16
110					6	6	10	13	4	4	1				44
100				1	8	14	21	9	5	3	1				62
90			1	6	9	15	14	8	2	2					57
80		1	5	15	21	22	9	1							74
70		1	13	16	10	2	1								43
60		1	3	3	2	2									11
50		2	6	1	1										10
40	1	1													2
30	1														1
Total	2	6	28	42	60	63	57	34	20	14	6	0	0	2	334

No. cases 334; S. D. (Binet) = 19.1; S. D. (Drawing) = 21.2; r = .741; P. E. = .016

51

The correlation with teachers' judgments of the intelligence of their pupils has been found to average about .44 for primary-grade classes. Significant correlations have also been found with a number of primary group tests.

INFLUENCE OF ARTISTIC TALENT ON THE SCORE

Attempt has been made to ascertain whether children who appear to possess special artistic talent are likely to make a higher score on the test than others of equal general ability who lack such gifts. A very unexpected difficulty was encountered here, that of locating the children. It is probable that in exceptional instances genuine artistic ability in drawing is shown by children in their early years, but these cases appear to be very rare. Kerschensteiner tells us of an eight-year-old boy who showed remarkable talent, especially in drawing horses. In recent years the work of Pamela Bianca (75), who held an exhibition in London at the age of eleven and at the Anderson Galleries in New York at the age of fourteen, has attracted much attention. At the New York exhibition, sketches were grouped according to the child's age at the time of drawing, beginning with seven years. Since many of these included drawings of the human figure, it was possible to score them at least roughly, although it chanced that in the earlier drawings only women and children were represented. The IQ as found by averaging the results of several drawings made at different ages was approximately 125, which is not out of proportion to the reported facts concerning her school progress and general ability. In spite of the really remarkable artistic qualities of these early drawings, the immaturity of thought was very evident. In only a few of the drawings in the first group was the nose shown, and ears did not appear until ten or eleven. The head, as a rule, was much exaggerated in size, as is likely to be the case in drawings of girls at that age. When one considers the num-

ber of child musicians who appear in our concert halls each
year, the dearth of child artists is rather surprising, and
suggests the explanation that artistic ability may be relatively late in its development. A study of the biographical
material found in Champlin's *Cyclopedia of Painters and
Paintings*, as compared with that in the *Cyclopedia of Music
and Musicians* by the same editor, tends to confirm this
view. In very few instances is it reported that the artists
showed unusual ability in drawing before the age of twelve
or thirteen, while a fair percentage of the musicians had not
only shown unmistakable talent, but had won some fame by
that time. In spite of careful search, both in connection
with this study and during a year spent as field worker in the
Stanford University gifted children survey, the writer has
been unable to locate a single child under the age of twelve
years whose drawings appeared to possess artistic merit of a
degree at all comparable to the musical genius occasionally
shown by children of this age. Examination of drawings
which make unusually high scores on the test leads to the
opinion that keen powers of analytic observation, coupled
with a good memory for details, are more potent factors in
producing high scores than is artistic ability in the ordinary
sense of the term.

INFLUENCE OF SPECIAL TRAINING ON THE SCORE

The question of the effect of special instruction in drawing
has been only partially answered. In the majority of school
systems the art instruction in the primary grades consists
almost entirely of simple decorative work, poster making,
paper cutting, and the like. No formal instruction in drawing the human figure is usual at this time. Repeated comparisons of the work of children who have had this type of
training, with that of children from schools in which no drawing at all is taught in the primary grades, have failed to show

any consistent differences between the performance of the two groups in drawing the human figure.

Direct training in drawing the human figure does, however, affect the test results to some extent. In San Francisco, first-grade children are taught to draw men, women, and children according to a set pattern which can, as a rule, be easily distinguished from the work of children who have not had this training. Many of these children, when given the drawing test by a person other than the teacher who ordinarily gave them their drawing lessons, reverted at once to the type of drawing which is usual for children of their age; and children in the second and third grades showed little or no effect of the training which they had had in first grade. The most marked effect of training was found with the Chinese children in the Oriental School, where, because of the marked language handicap, somewhat more time is devoted to drawing than is usual in other schools. Practically all these children kept to the stereotyped form which they had been taught, and the median IQ, when the drawings were scored according to the method used with untrained children, was 120. This is, of course, not at all in accordance with the actual ability of these children. In the American school which was tested very little effect upon the average IQ of the group could be observed, a class which had just completed the training actually ranking slightly below the entering class with whom the training had not yet begun. It is quite possible that the results with the Chinese children were due not only to more intensive but also to more protracted instruction, since the language handicap is such that the majority of these children spend two or more years in first grade, where the drawing of the human figure is taught.

Direct coaching *according to the method used for scoring the test* was given to one first-grade class. A control drawing was first obtained from each child. On each of the two following days a half-hour period was devoted to coaching on the drawing. The teacher, who knew the scoring method and had had considerable experience both in giving and scoring the test, dictated instructions to the children as they made their drawings, illustrated the method which they were to follow by means of the blackboard, pointed out errors in individual drawings and had them corrected, and in every possible way tried to increase the scores made. On the afternoon of the second day of coaching the test was again given in the usual way without help, and one week later an additional drawing was obtained.

Thirty-seven children were present on all five occasions. The median score made on the first or control drawing was 16.7 points; on the first drawing where coaching was given, 19.2 points; on the second drawing with coaching, 23.7 points. The median score on the drawings made four hours after the second coaching period was 22.5 points; a week later it had dropped to 20.7 points, which is a gain equivalent to one year of mental age above the control drawing. A comparison of the control with the final drawings showed that 70 per cent of the children had gained at least one point, while 8 per cent showed neither gain nor loss, and 22 per cent showed a slight loss. The standard error of estimate of a true score at this age is approximately 2 points. Fifty-four per cent of the children gained more than this amount; 40 per cent did not change their score by more than one standard error; and 6 per cent (2 cases) lost — one 3, the other 4 points.

These data show that, at least in the majority of cases, specific training in drawing the human figure does affect the score made on the test. There is no evidence that the kind of art training which is most commonly given in the primary grades, and which does not include formal instruction on the human figure, has any appreciable effect upon the score.

INFLUENCE OF OTHER FACTORS ON THE SCORE

Two other factors which may influence the test score need to be mentioned here. Children who have had little or no previous experience with a pencil should be given opportunity to gain such experience before they are given the test. Under ordinary conditions of modern life, practically all children have become sufficiently adapted to the use of pencil and paper by the time they have reached the age for entering first grade, but this is not always true with kindergarten children. For this reason it is recommended that, if the test is to be used with kindergarten children, the time for giving it should be deferred until at least a month after the opening of school.

The effect of self-consciousness, especially upon the work of older children, has been mentioned before. Children who have reached a period of development which causes them to be unduly critical of their work, not infrequently fail to do themselves justice in their drawing by very reason of their ability to recognize the difficulties involved. This is a factor which rarely enters into the work of the little children for whom the test has been designed, but it is one of the chief reasons for its decreasing usefulness with older children.

SEX DIFFERENCES

Table 8 (page 46) shows the distribution of intelligence quotients by age and sex separately for the Fresno, Rutherford, and Southern white groups. It will be noted that the girls rank somewhat higher than the boys at all ages except twelve, and that the variability of the boys is on the whole slightly greater than that of the girls.

The reason for the higher standing of the girls is almost certainly to be found in the method employed for standardizing the individual items of the test. It will be remembered that the criterion used was that of chronological age and school grade. An item was held to be a significant indication of mental development in proportion as it was found to differentiate between accelerated, normal, and retarded children of a given age. School statistics have almost invariably shown that girls, on the average, make more rapid progress through the grades than boys; that they are more often accelerated and less frequently retarded. An examination of the grade location of the 1671 children included in Table 8 shows that of the 888 boys, 69 or 7.8 per cent were accelerated; 550 or 61.9 per cent were in the grade corresponding to their chronological age; and 269 or 30.3 per cent were retarded. The corresponding figures for girls are 85 or 10.9 per cent accelerated, 538 or 68.7 per cent making normal progress, and 160 or 20.4 per cent retarded. Expressing these figures in another way, we find that 55.2 per cent of the accelerated children are girls and that 62.7 per cent of the retarded are boys, while the sexes are about equally represented in the group who have made normal progress. These figures agree fairly well with those published by Ayres (*159*), Lurton (*178*), and others.

As will be shown farther on, the drawings of boys and girls present very marked sex differences of a qualitative nature. It is obvious, then, that a method of standardization which takes the grade location of the subjects into consideration will inevitably result in giving greatest weight to those items or characteristics which occur most frequently among the children who are most advanced in school; and a sex difference in school progress will necessarily be accompanied by a sex difference in the average score earned on the drawing test.

It is, of course, possible that the æsthetic sense develops earlier with girls than with boys, and that their higher ratings may be partly accounted for on this basis. However, the work of previous investigators is not in harmony with such an hypothesis. Kerschensteiner (*57*), Ivanoff (*51*), Burt (*19*), and others who have based their classifications upon inspection of the drawing as a whole, report a marked sex difference in favor of the boys. This, taken in connection with the fact that artistic standards, as well as all other ideas of " better " or " worse," were disregarded in the construction of the present scale, makes it seem probable that some factor or factors other than a difference in drawing ability, as ordinarily defined, is responsible for the differences just noted. It has usually been assumed that the superior school progress made by girls is attributable to their greater docility and more studious habits rather than to any true intellectual difference between the sexes. An examination of the scale as a whole suggests that the child who is willing to persevere in the face of difficulties and to give careful attention to details is likely to make a somewhat higher score than another who, in a strict sense, may be said to have equal ability, but who is lacking in the characteristics just mentioned. It is possible that a slight superiority of girls over boys in traits such as these may account both for their more rapid progress in school and their higher average on the drawing test.

It is difficult to account for the nature of the qualitative differences shown in the drawings made by the two sexes. These differences become more apparent as the drawings increase in complexity ; but they are to be seen even in kindergarten drawings. The extent to which they exist is indicated by an experiment in which two hundred consecutive drawings, all scoring between 18 and 22 points (corresponding to a mental age range of seven and one half to eight and one half years), were ranked by the writer according to the degree of certainty which was felt in judging whether the drawing had been made by a boy or a girl. The drawings used belonged to a set which had been scored about a year previously, and had not been seen during the interval. No particular attention had been given to sex at the time of scoring, and results had been tabulated without reference to sex; hence it seems extremely unlikely that the ratings could have been in any way affected by memory. The drawings were rated on a seven-point scale. A rating of 1 was given if the experimenter felt "very certain" that the drawing had been made by a boy; of 7, for equal certainty that it had been made by a girl. Intermediate ratings from 2 to 6 were given for less positive judgments, a rating of 4 indicating that the sex characteristics were so evenly balanced that no judgment could be made. The distribution of ratings according to actual sex follows:

TABLE 11

DISTRIBUTION OF MASCULINITY RATINGS BY SEX

	1	2	3	4	5	6	7	N.	M.	S. D.
Boys . .	16	22	34	8	14	5	1	100	3.01 }	1.87
Girls . .	2	6	21	10	17	16	28	100	4.94 }	

The bi-serial coefficient of correlation is .646. The correlation would have been somewhat higher if drawings by older children had been used, and would have been slightly lower with younger children. However, the characteristics are of the same nature at whatever age they appear. They are more prominent in the drawings of older children because of the greater number of items which these drawings contain.

It is conceivable that a careful study of qualitative differences such as these might bring out facts which would be of decided value in the analysis of specific mental functions and of individual interests and personality traits. Such a study, however, is beyond the scope of the present investigation.

Nevertheless, a few suggestive points have been brought out which are offered for what they may be worth.

It was felt that it would be of interest to tabulate some of the more striking differences, and see to what extent they might appear to correspond to what is known in respect to the relative interests and abilities of boys and girls. For this purpose a group of one hundred drawings by children of each sex, all scoring between 22 and 26 points, were selected at random from ten different localities representing a wide range of social status and racial stock. The subjects included negroes from Tennessee, white children from Louisiana, Italians from San Jose, Mexicans from Los Angeles, Indians from the Hoopa Valley Reservation, Armenians from Fresno, Chinese and Japanese from several California towns, Jewish children from San Jose and Fresno, and two groups of American children, of which one was selected from California schools largely of foreign population, the other from two very wealthy neighborhoods in New Jersey.

The cases listed in the table on the opposite page are representative of the sex differences found. Since there were exactly 100 children of each sex, the number of cases may also be regarded as percentages.

A number of other characteristics were noted, but those in the table will serve as examples. At first sight the points mentioned appear too trivial to merit attention. However, when one considers that the same types of sex differences are found in the work of children from such widely separated localities and social antecedents as those in the experiment under consideration, and that they may also be observed in the drawings which have been published by European investigators (see especially Kerschensteiner and Rouma), it is hard to escape the conclusion that, however unimportant these matters may seem, they probably carry a profound meaning, had we but the wisdom to understand it. For

	NUMBER OF DRAWINGS SHOWING CHARACTERISTIC	
	Boys	Girls
Masculine characteristics:		
At least head and feet shown in profile, and in same direction	58	36
Some accessory characteristic present, as pipe, cane, umbrella, house, or scenery	21	9
Trousers transparent	12	3
Heel present	53	37
Figure represented as walking or running . . .	20	7
Arms reaching below knee	11	3
Necktie shown	25	14
Feminine characteristics:		
Nose represented only by two dots	7	28
Feet less than $\frac{1}{20}$ total body length	4	16
Eyes showing two or more of the following details: brow, lashes, pupil, iris	1	11
Hair very smooth or neatly parted	13	34
"Cupid's bow" mouth	1	7
Cheeks shown	1	7
Trousers flaring at base	6	21
Head larger than trunk	9	17
Arm length not greater than head length . . .	11	26
Curly hair	2	7
Legs not more than $\frac{1}{4}$ trunk length	2	12

example, a difference in the interest taken in physical activity may be the reason for the greater tendency of the boys to exaggerate the size of the feet and the length of the arms and legs, as compared with the girls' tendency to minimize these parts. This is in line with the fact that the drawings of the boys more often show the figure in action. It is quite possible that it is this desire to express movement which leads to the characteristic change from the full-face to the profile position which has been so universally noted by students of children's drawings. In my collection, this change takes place appreciably earlier and more generally with boys than with girls.

The girls are inclined to exaggerate the size of the head and the trunk, and, more especially, of the eyes. It is not a very uncommon circumstance for a girl to draw the eyes larger than the feet, while boys are likely to make the feet larger than the entire head. In general, however, the sense of proportion displayed by the boys is decidedly better than that shown by the girls, while girls excel in the number of items and the amount of detail with which they are shown. Figures 55–58 (page 140) are examples of markedly " feminine " drawings; Figures 59–61 (page 142), of drawings that are markedly " masculine."

Occasionally a child is found whose drawings strongly resemble those of the opposite sex. The significance of this has not been determined. It is interesting to note that out of fourteen drawings by children who had been diagnosed as psychopathic at Lane Hospital, San Francisco, seven were of this type.

INDICATIONS OF PSYCHOPATHY

The work of Kurbitz (*125*), Reja (*128, 129*), Rogues de Fursac (*123*), and others has shown that in many instances unmistakable evidence of the disintegration of mental function can be observed in the drawings made by the insane. At how early a period in the development of mental disorders these indications first appear is not known, but if the modern theory which ascribes a considerable proportion of these disorders to an original instability in the nervous organism be correct, then it is not impossible that a type of performance which is so closely related to the mental life of the individual as is spontaneous drawing, may sometimes reveal such instability before it has manifested itself to any marked degree in everyday behavior.

In the course of the present study it was found that in a small proportion of drawings, qualitative differences may be observed of a type which cannot readily be accounted for. These differences are often of so subtle a nature as to render description very difficult, but they may be classified roughly as follows:

1. " Verbalist " type. Drawings containing a large amount of detail but comparatively few ideas. Figure 62 is an example. See Mateer (*126*).

2. " Individual response " type. Drawings containing features which are inexplicable to any one except the child himself. See Figure 65. Compare Kent and Rosanoff (*176*).

3. Drawings showing evidence of the flight of ideas, as when hair is shown only on one side of the head, or when one ear but not the other has been drawn. See Rouma (*129*).

4. Uneven mental development, as indicated by unusual combinations of primitive and mature characteristics in a single drawing. (Analogous to " scatter " on the Stanford-Binet.)

In one school with an enrollment of about 450 children, nine drawings were found which showed one or more of these characteristics to a fairly marked degree. This is 2 per cent of the total. It was felt that it would be of interest to see whether these children appeared to differ from their class-mates in temperament and emotional poise. For this pur-pose a list of fifty adjectives and phrases descriptive of personality traits was prepared, using only words in such common use that the average elementary teacher might be expected to understand them. Twenty-five of the words (such as " unstable," " prone to worry," etc.) were chosen with a view to their possible significance in indicating psycho-pathic tendencies; the remaining twenty-five were the oppo-sites of these words. Copies of the list were sent to the teachers of each of the nine children, together with the follow-ing directions:

" Below is a list of fifty words and descriptive phrases. Please read through the list and *underline* each expression which, in your opinion, seems to apply to the child named here . . . ."

The two lists of words had been combined so that the undesirable phrases were distributed irregularly throughout the total list. Each of the nine children who had been selected was paired off against another child from the same class, of the same sex, and as nearly as possible of the same age, whose drawing was free from the characteristics under consideration, and the same questionnaire was filled out for these children as well. The basis of selection was not known to the teachers.

The average number of words underlined for the selected group was 12.3; for the control group, 11.8. This difference is probably of no significance. Since there were only nine cases in each group, the total number of underlinings for any single word was too small to make formal statistical treatment worth while. The following lists merely show which words were underlined more frequently for the selected group than for the control group, and vice versa. Words not underlined at all, or underlined as often for one group as for the other, have been omitted.

A. WORDS SHOWING NO OVERLAPPING BETWEEN GROUPS

UNDERLINED MORE FREQUENTLY FOR THE SELECTED GROUP			UNDERLINED MORE FREQUENTLY FOR THE CONTROL GROUP		
	FREQUENCIES			FREQUENCIES	
	Selected Group	Control Group		Selected Group	Control Group
Placid	4	0	Practical	0	3
Over-sensitive . .	3	0			
Courageous [1] . . .	2	0			
Prone to worry . .	2	0			
Muscles twitch . .	2	0			
Apathetic	1	0			
Cries without cause	1	0			
Passionate temper .	1	0			

B. WORDS SHOWING UNEQUAL OVERLAPPING

	Selected	Control		Selected	Control
Concentrates poorly	5	1	Cheerful	1	4
Absent-minded . .	5	2	Good-natured . .	3	6
Timid	4	2	Calm	1	4
Unstable	4	2	Good self-control .	1	4
Flighty	4	2	Shows good common sense . . .	4	7
Boastful	4	2	Reasonable . . .	2	5
Stubborn	3	1	Well poised . . .	1	3
Optimistic . . .	2	1	Happy disposition .	1	3
Easily depressed .	3	2	Popular with other children . . .	1	3
Dreamy	3	2	Nervous	2	3
Peculiar	5	4	Dependable . . .	2	3
Restless	3	2	Active	3	4
Free from nervousness	3	2	Stable	1	2
Healthy	5	4	Well balanced . .	1	2

Through the kindness of Dr. Mary Layman of the Children's Clinic at Lane Hospital, San Francisco, drawings were also secured from fourteen children examined at the clinic who appeared to show psychopathic tendencies. The characteristics which have been referred to were much less evident in this group than the above findings might lead one to expect. The most noticeable characteristic observed was the large proportion of drawings of a type usually made by children

[1] In one case with the note "too much so" added by the teacher.

of the opposite sex.   Seven out of the fourteen cases showed this peculiarity, which is greatly in excess of the proportion usually found.   (See Table 11 on page 59.)   The motor coördination displayed, considering the group as a whole, was decidedly below average (compare Mateer), and there was more than the usual tendency to combine primitive and mature elements in a single drawing.   Apart from these facts, no significant differences could be observed between this group of drawings and those made by normal children of the same mental age.   It must, of course, be remembered that no formal analysis has been made of these drawings, the only method of rating used being the subjective impression gained by means of a rather extensive acquaintance with the drawings of unselected children.   Obviously such a method is subject to a very wide margin of error.

The facts herein reported are by no means intended to convey the impression that the writer is able to diagnose psychopathic tendencies in children by means of a drawing. Certainly no such claim is justified.   It is believed, however, that by an investigation carried out along the lines which have been indicated a method of scoring might be derived which would throw new light upon eccentricities of mental functioning during childhood.   For this reason the points brought out by the very crude experiment which has been described are deemed worthy of presentation.

CHAPTER FOUR

THE PSYCHOLOGICAL INTERPRETATION OF CHILDREN'S DRAWINGS

AN attempt to trace the development of the mental processes which govern the child's first attempts at representative drawing leads us back to the period of very early infancy. The mental life of the new-born child can be little more than an unorganized series of sensations which force themselves upon the developing consciousness with greater or less insistence, according to the intensity of the physical stimulus and the immediate condition of the receiving organism. Little by little, however, certain groups of sensations begin to single themselves out from the others. Vaguely but surely the child begins to differentiate between his mother and other persons with whom he is brought into contact, between familiar and strange surroundings, etc. These first associations and recognitions are perhaps more nearly related to the conditioned reflex than to the conscious reasoning of later life; yet in them we can trace the beginnings of analysis, of differentiation and comparison, which, as will be shown, are among the basic processes in the type of activity with which we are concerned.

From the recognition of individual objects the child progresses by imperceptible stages to the recognition of classes of objects, and, later on, to the recognition of pictorial representations of objects. Perez (91) and Darwin (29) considered that the time when objects seen in a mirror are clearly recognized as images, and not as the objects themselves (as is shown by the child's turning away from the mirror to look for the source of the reflection), marks one of the earliest stages in the development of the ability to recognize objects in pictures. This development is characterized by an increasing ability to analyze, to abstract certain elements from the total impression made by an object, and to reconstruct the whole in terms of those parts which experience has shown to be essential to it.   The infant of a few weeks can recognize his mother only through the combined action of a large number of sensory impressions — visual, tactual, auditory, and, it may be, olfactory as well.   Little by little he becomes able to substitute a single group of sensations for the total, so that the sight of his mother or the sound of her voice is alone sufficient to awaken the response which was formerly elicited only by actual contact.   By a like process of abstraction and substitution, not the less important because it is for the most part unconscious, the child becomes able to dispense with more and more of the usual concomitants of the sensory impression and to replace them by centrally initiated equivalents, so that eventually a small photograph of his mother is sufficient to arouse recognition, in spite of the difference in size, the absence of color, and the changes in ocular accommodation incident to the elimination of the third dimension.

We are accustomed to speak of this type of recognition as " association by similarity."   More precisely defined, it is association by the similarity of certain parts or elements, in spite of the dissimilarity of other parts.   Many writers on primitive art have called attention to the importance of this factor in the development of representative drawing.   A number of instances are extant, especially among the prehistoric rock drawings which have been found in the caves of Southern France, in which advantage has been taken of some natural fissure or discoloration in the rock itself to lessen the labor of drawing or carving — the fissure serving as a partial outline, and the remainder of the drawing being added by the artist.   Koch-Grünberg (*141*) has shown that in certain South American petroglyphs the grooves which have been worn in the rocks by fishing lines have been used in this way. Similar instances have been found in primitive sculpture, especially in wood carving, where a peculiarly shaped knot or twisted branch frequently appears to have served as the original suggestion for the work.

In the early drawings of very young children a circumstance somewhat analogous to the foregoing has frequently been reported. The child whose work has previously consisted only of random scribbling suddenly sees a resemblance between the incoherent lines obtained by chance and some known object. He tries to complete or to perfect the resemblance, and in this way the first real attempts at graphic expression come into being. It is not necessary to suppose that these associations are entirely spontaneous in all instances. It is probable that in many cases they are directly aroused by the questions or comments of older persons, and it can hardly be doubted that the child's previous acquaintance with pictures is a factor of much importance. It must be remembered, however, that these external circumstances can be effective only in case the mind has developed to a stage at which it can profit by them; otherwise they are comparable to the many "inadequate stimuli" of the physical world, whereof the inadequacy consists, not in the stimuli themselves, but in the non-adaptation of the organism to their reception. While variations in external conditions may retard or accelerate the development of graphic expression to some degree, especially in the first stages, the conditions of modern life are such that few children fail to grasp the idea of pictorial representation because of its unfamiliarity.

An experiment which appears to indicate that "association by similarity" plays an important part even in decorative art is reported by Paulsson (90). Paulsson is of the opinion that the first impulse toward graphic expression has its origin in the desire for emotional outlet, the pleasure derived from the objectification of emotion. In order to determine the nature of the specific stimulus which serves to direct this impulse toward a particular type of performance, two experiments were carried out by Paulsson under carefully controlled conditions. Adult subjects were used in both instances, most of whom were accustomed to psychological experimentation. Several artists were included. In the first experiment, in which nine subjects took part, a series of ten ink blots were exposed, one at a time, for a brief interval. After each exposure the subjects were told to draw from memory what they had seen, and to " make their drawings beautiful." It was found that each interpreted the blots according to his individual interests. A doctor drew one of them as a section of the spinal cord; an art theorist made them into an example of his art theory; etc. But little similarity could be observed between the drawings of the same blot as made by different subjects. In the second experiment, in which fourteen subjects took part, a tachistoscope was used and two hundred ink blots were shown, but the subjects were told that they need draw only as many of them as they liked. Again the instructions were to " make them beautiful." Introspective results showed that in this experiment only those blots were drawn which suggested a meaning of some sort to the observer. In the actual drawing everything was subordinated to this meaning — unrelated elements being minimized or omitted, while other parts, which furnished, as it were, the cue to the idea, were emphasized. From these data Paulsson concludes that it is the meaning which furnishes the aim. " It is the meaning, therefore, that guides the graphic ' structures ' in their development from the primitive schematic stages to the highest manifestations of the artistic mind."

Albien (1), in a somewhat similar experiment in which unfamiliar geometrical figures were used as the stimuli and the subjects were children of from nine to eighteen years of age, obtained much the same results. He decided that directed observation and analysis, followed by apperception and assimilation of many partial elements into a unified whole, are the primary factors in the ability to reproduce the figure. Observation itself is less important than the relationships observed. It would seem that " relationship," as he uses the term, is somewhat analogous to " meaning " as used by Paulsson.

Meumann (78) has given us a very useful summary of the factors which tend to produce inability or defective ability in drawing. He classifies these factors as follows:

1. Analytic observation is lacking, either because of inability to analyze or unwillingness to observe.
2. Visual imagery is defective or transitory.
3. Eye-hand coördination is defective.
4. The imperfection of the actual work interferes with the memory image as the drawing progresses.
5. Related drawing schemes are lacking.
6. There is inability to understand and portray three-dimensional space; inability to escape from the childish idea that all that exists must be shown.
7. Manual skill is defective.

A later study by Meumann (79) analyzes the drawing act from the positive standpoint. He concludes that it is dependent upon three groups of factors, as follows:

1. Visual activity, as eye movements which underlie appreciation of distance, direction, etc.
2. Activity of eye and hand; accuracy of motor coördination.
3. Apperceptive ideas, involving a strong intellectual element.

Hence, he adds, there must be:

1. Association of eye and hand movements.
2. Association of visual memory and hand movements.
3. Association of these elements and apperceptive factors.

It should be noted that Meumann's experiments were carried on with children of grammar school age and had to do only with drawing from copy or directly from the object itself, followed by work in immediate recall. His analysis, therefore, has only partial application to the present experiment, that of drawing a man without model or copy and with no suggestions apart from those arising spontaneously in the child mind from the concept which has previously been formed. Under these circumstances the performance is seen to be only indirectly dependent upon visual activity (assuming, of course, reasonably normal visual acuity), the importance of eye-hand coördination is greatly lessened, and the intellectual element becomes the predominating factor in determining the result. As has been said before, drawing of this sort is for little children a language, a form of expression. Art it may be called, but its purpose is not primarily æsthetic; nor is it, in the beginning, a simple matter of the reproduction of a visual image. Repeated experiments have demonstrated the truth of the saying that " the child draws what he knows, not what he sees."

One of the simplest, as well as the most convincing, of these experiments is that carried out by Professor A. B. Clark of Stanford University (*24*). Clark had several hundred children draw an apple with a hatpin run through it. The hatpin entered the apple on the side turned toward the children, and emerged on the side turned away from them. To none of the children could it be seen as entering or leaving exactly at the edge. When the drawings were examined, however, it was found that the younger children had, in almost all instances, drawn the hatpin extending straight through the apple from side to side and visible throughout its length. Those slightly older had realized that the portion of the hatpin which was within the apple could not be visible, but had paid no attention to its apparent point of entrance. In drawings of this type the pin stopped at the outline of the apple on one side, and began again at a roughly corresponding point on the opposite side. Only in the upper grades was it found that the visual image of the object actually before the children had served any other purpose than that of giving the cue for the idea; given the idea, the nature of the drawing was no longer dependent upon the image immediately present.

Kerschensteiner found no perceptible difference between the memory or, to speak more precisely, the " concept" drawings of little children and those made when a model was placed before them. Children who were accustomed to draw the human figure in full face continued to do so even when the model was placed in the profile position.

It seems evident, then, that an explanation of the psychological functions which underlie the spontaneous drawing of little children must go beyond the fields of simple visual imagery and eye-hand coördination and take account of the higher thought processes. It has been said that the ability to recognize objects in pictures, an ability which must obviously precede any real attempt to represent objects by means of pictures, is dependent upon the ability to form associations by the similarity of certain elements which are common both to the picture and to the object, in spite of the dissimilarity of other elements. Analysis and abstraction are clearly involved, but only the final result is present in consciousness. The three-year-old child who recognizes the photograph of his mother cannot tell you by what means he is able to do so, and even the adult finds such a task difficult. In order to represent objects by means of pictures there must be, however, a conscious analysis of the process, of the intermediate steps by means of which the desired result is to be obtained. It is necessary to select from out the total impression those elements or features which appear to be characteristic or essential. This analysis must be followed or accompanied by observation of relationships. The relationships to be observed are of two kinds, quantitative and spatial. The former determine the proportion, the latter the position, of the various parts of the drawing with reference to each other. Very great individual differences are found among children with respect to the extent to which these functions keep pace with each other. In general it may be said that the brighter the child, the more closely is his analysis of a figure followed by an appreciation of the relationships prevailing between the elements which are brought out by his analysis. Backward children, on the other hand, are likely to be particularly slow in grasping abstract ideas of this or any other kind. They analyze a figure to some extent, and by this means are able to set down some of its elements in a graphic fashion, but the ability to combine these elements into an organized whole is likely to be defective and in some instances seems to be almost entirely lacking. It is this inability to analyze, to form abstract ideas, to relate facts, that is largely responsible for the bizarre effects so frequently found among the drawings of backward children — the "*Zusammenhangenlosigkeit*" to which Kerschensteiner has called attention.

If we accept the theory that a child's drawing of an object during this early, or, as it has been called, "pre-artistic," period is dependent primarily upon his concept of that object rather than upon immediate visual imagery or artistic appreciation, it becomes possible to explain the fact that the developmental changes which take place in children's drawings do not remain fixed from the time of their first appearance. Instead, any new characteristic usually goes through a longer or shorter period of fluctuation, during which time it is sometimes shown, sometimes not. Only gradually does it become a consistent feature of all the drawings which the child makes. This fluctuation is, however, a necessary accompaniment of any intellectual manifestation which is in reality continuous, but which is measured only in discrete steps. Memory for digits is an example. There is no sudden leap from the stage in which only five digits can be remembered to that in which it is always possible to remember six. On the contrary, it will be found that the person who can always, or practically always, remember five digits after a single reading will occasionally be able to remember six, or, more rarely, even as many as seven. The same principle holds good in children's drawings. The progress from the simple concepts which govern the crude productions of the four-year-old, to the comparatively complex and highly developed ideas of the ten-year-old, is indicated in the drawings by a series of rather marked changes. At first these changes appear only sporadically; later on they tend to become fixed. When a child, whose drawing of the human figure has consisted only of head, legs, and trunk, first begins to add the arms, he does not do so invariably. As his concept develops, however, the arms tend more and more to become an essential part of it, with the consequence that they are shown more and more frequently until a period is reached when the child no longer regards his drawing as complete without them. It may thus be said that at any given time a child's drawing will consist of two parts — the first part embracing those characteristics which have already become an integral part of his concept of the object drawn, and consequently appear invariably; the second part including the elements which are in process of becoming integrated and are therefore shown with more or less irregularity. The frequency with which any given characteristic tends to appear is a function of the extent to which it has become integrated into the developing concept, and a measure of the weight which should be given to it as an index of concept development.

The " frequent retrogressions to an inferior stage " which Rouma finds characteristic of the drawings of backward children are easily explained if we assume that the integration of the various elements into the total concept takes place at a less rapid rate with backward than with normal children. A similar explanation would account for the qualitative differences found in drawings made by children in special classes for defectives, which Burt (*19*, page 326) has described in the following paragraph:

Compared with drawings from ordinary schools, those obtained in the special schools resemble the work of children from two to three years younger. . . . There are, however, in the drawings of defectives special differences in kind and character, as well as a general deficiency in degree, so that it is usually possible to distinguish the drawing of an older defective from that of a younger normal child. These differences well deserve study. They may, perhaps, be most briefly epitomized by saying that the drawings of the defective are apt to include inconsistent features, characterizing stages of development which among normals are distinct and even remote.

It is evident that the child does not show in his drawing all the facts which he knows about the object, but only those which to him are so essential or characteristic that they occur to him spontaneously without suggestion from outside sources. A three-year-old child will point to his hair when asked to do so, but 50 per cent of nine-year-old children are entirely content to draw the human figure without a vestige of hair, although these same children include in their drawings such non-essential features as flashing scarfpins, elaborate hat bands, pipes, canes, etc. The problem which the child has to meet is primarily one of selection, of determining which ones of a vast number of items really furnish the key to the situation. Knowledge of a fact does not in itself guarantee that this fact shall be shown in a drawing; its importance must also have been evaluated. Terman (*188*) has shown that the majority of seven-year-old children *know* the number of their fingers when the question is put to them; yet only 31 per cent of unselected seven-year-olds show the correct number in their drawings when no suggestion is made. The difference can hardly be due to technical difficulty; at least it is hard to see why it should be any more difficult to draw five fingers than to draw four or six, or, as occurred in the case of one kindergarten child, twenty-nine on one hand and thirty-six on the other! Carelessness, in the sense of lack of appreciation of the importance of details, is undoubtedly one of the factors involved; yet when one notices the care with which some of these drawings have been finished, and the effort which has apparently been expended upon them, it appears evident that carelessness, in the ordinary sense of the term, is not an adequate explanation for the discrepancy in the findings by the two methods. The determining factor appears to be the presence or absence of the definite stimulus, " How many? " In the one instance, that which is measured is the memory of a particular percept; in the other, the integration of that percept into the concept of which it is a part. By referring to Table 1 (point 10 *b*), it will be seen that as large a proportion of accelerated six-year-olds as of retarded ten-year-olds have been found to show the correct number of fingers in their drawings of the human figure. This indicates that the ability to evaluate the importance of facts such as the foregoing is one of the elements in determining school success.

It is interesting to compare the above facts with certain unpublished vocabulary data collected by Mr. L. G. Schussman of Stanford University. Mr. Schussman had about one hundred children of the eighth and ninth grades write definitions of a number of words, choosing for this purpose words in such common use as to make it highly unlikely that any of the children would ever have had occasion to look them up in a dictionary. The failure to give proper evaluation to

facts which were almost certainly well known was very evident in the nature of the responses received. The word
mother, for example, was variously defined as " a female,"
" a parent," " a woman who takes care of her children," etc.
It may almost be taken for granted that eighth and ninth
grade children know, and if specifically questioned could
state, that a mother is not simply a female or a parent, but a
female parent. They know that a father is also a parent,
and in ordinary conversation they never confuse the two.
Nevertheless, they are entirely satisfied with a definition
which includes only one, or perhaps neither, of the two
essential characteristics of an adequate " mother " concept
— parenthood and femaleness. There is a distinct difference
between knowledge of facts and appreciation of their relative
significance.

Turning again to the specific problem under consideration
— that of the child who is given the task of drawing a picture
of a man without outside aid or suggestion — we see that the
psychological processes involved may be classified as follows :

1. *Association by similarity.* The child sees a resemblance
between a series of lines on paper and the concrete object
which is represented by them. This is the preliminary stage,
which must precede any active attempt at representation on
the part of the child himself.

2. *Analysis into its component parts* of the object to be
drawn.

3. *Evaluation of these parts* and selection of those which
appear to be essential or characteristic. This process is
largely an unconscious one as far as the child is concerned,
but it is significant, since it is determined by the nature of his
interests and by his fundamental habits of thought.

4. *Analysis of spatial relationships; of relative position.*

5. *Judgments of quantitative relationships; of relative
proportion.*

6. Through *further process of abstraction*, reduction and simplification of the several parts into graphic outlines.

7. *Coördination of eye and hand movements* in the drawing act.

8. *Adaptability;* the capacity to adjust the drawing scheme to the new features which are added from time to time as the concept develops.

Considered as a whole, the process is quite analogous to that described by James in his classic distinction between " reasoning " and " common associative thinking." Of the former he says:

It contains analysis and abstraction. Whereas the merely empirical thinker stares at a fact in its entirety, . . . the reasoner breaks it up and notices one of its separate attributes. This attribute he takes to be the essential part of the whole fact before him. . . . Reasoning may then be very well defined as the substitution of parts and their implications or consequences for wholes. And the art of the reasoner will consist of two stages:

First, *sagacity*, or the ability to discover what part, M, lies embedded in the whole which is before him.

Second, *learning*, or the ability to recall promptly M's consequences, concomitants, or implications.

In a footnote James adds the following:

To be sagacious is to be a good observer. J. S. Mill has a passage which is so much in the spirit of the text that I cannot forbear to quote it. "The observer is not he who merely sees the thing which is before his eyes, but he who sees what parts that thing is composed of. . . . One person, from inattention or from attending only in the wrong place, overlooks half of what he sees; another sets down much more than he sees, confounding it with what he imagines or with what he infers; another takes notes of the *kind* of all the circumstances, but being inexpert in estimating their degree leaves the *quantity* of each vague and uncertain; another sees, indeed, the whole, but makes such an awkward division of it into parts, throwing things into one mass which require to be separated, and separating things which might more conveniently have been considered as one, that the result is much the same, sometimes even worse, than as if no analysis had been attempted at all."

In the foregoing pages an attempt has been made to point out some of the psychological factors involved in the spontaneous drawing of young children, and to show their relationship to general intellectual development. It is believed that these drawings afford a means for the study of mental growth which is of value both to the practical educator and to the psychologist. The former will find that they throw additional light on the factors which govern school success and failure; the latter will find them useful in the analysis of specific mental functions and in the study of the development of conceptual thinking during early childhood. It is felt that the present experiment, which has dealt chiefly with the intellectual side, has by no means exhausted the possibilities which these drawings possess for the study of child development. On the contrary, it is the writer's opinion that, if properly understood, they would contribute much to our knowledge of child interests and personality traits. It is hoped that the experiment which has been described will point the way to further research into this very fundamental type of childish expression.

CHAPTER FIVE

SUMMARY AND CONCLUSIONS

1. THE experiment under consideration had as its object the study of the intellectual factors involved in the spontaneous drawing of young children, and it has involved the construction of a scale to be used in the measurement of these factors. This scale is based on drawings of the human figure.

2. As finally developed, the scale consists of fifty-one points, or units of measurement. The points were derived by means of (a) the observation of differences which appeared to be characteristic of the performances of children at successive ages or school grades; (b) the formulation of objective definitions or descriptions of these differences; and (c) their statistical validation based on a comparison between the performances of children of different ages, and also between the performances of children who were accelerated in school and those who were retarded. While no claim of absolute accuracy or finality of rating is made for the scale, the results obtained indicate that it forms a serviceable test of intellectual development, which is useful both for making comparisons between groups, and as a supplement to the usual type of intelligence test in the study of individual cases. It is particularly suitable for investigating the mentality of children from foreign homes or of deaf children.

3. The probable error of estimate of an IQ is approximately 5.4 points at all ages from five to ten years.

4. Partial correlation treatment shows that the test makes a significant contribution to a prognosis of school success which is independent of that given by Army Alpha, Trabue Completion, or a teacher's judgment.

81

5. The average correlation with Stanford-Binet mental age is .763 for ages 4 to 12 taken separately. The range of talent included was somewhat greater than is likely to be found within the limits of a single class or school, but is perhaps comparable to that which would be yielded by the total school enrollment of an average city.

6. Significant correlations have also been obtained with other standardized intelligence tests.

7. The correlation with teachers' judgments of ability was found to be .444 within the first three grades; but in grades above the third, the correlation with teachers' judgments was too low to be significant.

8. The test results can be influenced by special coaching in drawing the human figure, but they appear to be relatively unaffected by the type of art instruction ordinarily given in the primary grades.

9. Artistic ability is practically a negligible factor at these ages, as far as influencing the score is concerned.

10. Tentative experimentation suggests the possibility of devising a method of scoring drawings in such a way as to throw light on functional mental disorders, but such a method has not yet been developed.

11. Girls make a slightly better showing on the test than do boys. The most marked sex differences, however, are of a qualitative rather than a quantitative nature. These differences might well repay further study.

12. It is believed that the test throws considerable light on the development of conceptual thinking in young children.

PART TWO

CHAPTER SIX

Test Procedure and Directions for Scoring

TEST PROCEDURE

Each child should be provided with a pencil and a test blank. Crayons should *not* be used, but the large " beginner's " pencils may be used if the children are more accustomed to them. Before beginning, see that all books and pictures are put away, so that there will be no opportunity for copying.

The following instructions are then given:

" On these papers I want you to make a picture of a man. Make the very best picture that you can. Take your time and work very carefully. I want to see whether the boys and girls in —————— school can do as well as those in other schools. Try very hard and see what good pictures you can make."

As the drawings are being made, the examiner should stroll about the room to see that instructions are being followed, and encourage, by means of a little judicious praise, any one who seems to need it. In doing this it is best to avoid calling attention to the work of any individual child; rather, let the comments be of a general nature, such as, " These drawings are fine; you boys and girls are doing very well," etc. Never make adverse comments or criticism, and under no circumstances should a child's attention be called to any errors or omissions in his work, however gross they may be. Answer all questions by saying, " Do it whatever way you think is best."

The importance of avoiding every kind of suggestion cannot be overemphasized. Not only must the examiner himself refrain from all remarks which could influence the nature of the drawings (the only exception to this rule is noted in a following paragraph), but he must see to it that no suggestions come from the children. They should not be permitted to hold up their drawings for admiration or comment in such a way that other children may see them, or to make audible remarks about their work. If permitted to do so, little children are very likely to accompany their performance by a running fire of description, such as, " I'm giving my man a soldier hat," " Mine's going to have a big, long pipe," etc. While it is true that these comments are most likely to have to do with appurtenances which do not affect the score, there is danger that a child who attempts to carry out such suggestions may thereby have his attention so distracted from his original concept as to cause him to forget some of the essential parts of his drawing in his interest in this new, and probably unimportant, detail.

The examiner must not, however, lose sight of this fact: *It is essential for the validity of the test that each child make the best effort of which he is capable.* To secure such effort, a cheerful, sympathetic attitude must be adopted throughout. The child who is bursting with eagerness to tell about his drawing must be suppressed, it is true, but never in such a way as to dampen his enthusiasm. A firm but good-natured " No one must tell about his picture now. Wait until everybody has finished," will usually dispose of such cases without affecting the general interest or disturbing the rapport which should exist between examiner and children.

There is no time limit for the test, but little children rarely take more than five or ten minutes. If one or two children are slower than the rest, it is best to collect papers from those who have finished, and allow them to go on with their regular work while the slower workers are finishing.

The following special circumstances should be noted: (1) It sometimes happens that through erasure or other accident a child may spoil his drawing. In such cases he should always be given a fresh sheet and be allowed to try again. All such instances should be noted on the back of the sheet. (2) In grades above the second (rarely below), it will occasionally be found that a child has drawn a bust picture only. When it is evident that this has been the intention, a fresh paper should be given and the child told to " make the whole man." Both papers should be preserved for comparison.

GENERAL INSTRUCTIONS FOR SCORING

While the test may be given by the regular classroom teacher, it is better to make other provision for the scoring. In school systems where there is a special department to look after the tests and measurements, all scoring should be done by some member of this department. Where no such arrangement exists, a special teacher, preferably one who has had experience along this line, may learn to do the scoring. The task of learning how to score is not an especially difficult one for an intelligent person who is willing to devote the necessary time and patience to a thorough mastery of the directions given; but it cannot be emphasized too strongly that such study is imperative, if results are to be of any value. Because of the amount of time necessary to learn the scoring method, it is obviously unwise to divide the task of scoring among too many workers. The gain both in speed and accuracy which comes with practice is enormous — so much so that an experienced scorer can readily attain a speed of from forty to fifty papers an hour, although in the beginning he may not have been able to score more than five or ten an hour. The following general instructions should be noted:

1. As a preliminary exercise, the beginner should check through the scoring of the illustrative drawings shown on pages 112–161. There are two series of these drawings.

The first series should be used as a guide for study; the second as a test exercise. The student is advised to read the directions for scoring the different points very carefully, referring, as he does so, to the drawings in Series I. He should note in each case whether a plus or minus score has been given for the point under consideration, and endeavor to fix clearly in his mind the principles which govern the scoring. If he has had little previous experience in work of this kind, it may be well for him to go over the rules a second or a third time before proceeding to any independent work. As soon as he feels that the rules have been thoroughly mastered and that the scoring of the drawings in Series I is well understood, the next step is to score the drawings in Series II without reference to the standard scoring of these drawings which is given on pages 160–161. If his total error is found to be not more than one or two points, it will ordinarily be safe for him to begin regular work in scoring, provided that he proceed rather carefully at first and refer to the guide whenever there is doubt as to the scoring of any point.

2. Time will be saved and the scoring will be rendered appreciably more accurate if special drawing sheets[1] with spaces for recording the scores on the separate points by their key numbers are used. After a reasonable amount of practice, these numbers will serve as sufficient cues for the scorer so that continual reference to the manual becomes unnecessary. The scoring can then be done much more rapidly, without the danger of overlooking or omitting points which is likely to result from complete reliance upon the memory. This also makes possible the rechecking of scores, point by point, a procedure which is always desirable in the beginning or when inexperienced scorers are used.

3. In practice, drawings will occasionally be found which the scorer is unable to interpret. The most common types

[1] These are supplied with orders for *Goodenough Intelligence Test*, published by World Book Company, Yonkers-on-Hudson, New York.

of these bizarre drawings have been described in the text, together with notes as to their scoring. While it is not to be hoped that all the unusual forms which will be met with have been described, nevertheless, since a selection has been made from several thousand drawings made by children of widely separated localities and social antecedents, it is probable that a basis will have been afforded for the settlement of many of the ordinary difficulties. In all cases where doubt exists as to what has been intended by any particular portion of a drawing, it is well to consult the child, if this is possible, and to score the drawing in accordance with his reply, bearing in mind that special requirements as to the manner of representing any particular item must be met in these cases as well as in others.

4. All computations should be checked carefully. Age should be taken to the nearest month, scores should be transmuted into mental age equivalents by reference to the table on page 39, and the IQ found by dividing the mental age by the chronological age.

5. If, as sometimes happens with young children, more than one drawing has been made, select for the child's rating the one which makes the highest score. This will ordinarily be the first one made, since in subsequent drawings there is likely to be a slight falling off of interest and effort. In some cases, however, the second drawing shows improvement over the first, usually because of the fact that the child noticed some error or omission in his first drawing and drew the second by way of correction. In any case, the best drawing is the one to be credited. It is not permissible, in such cases, to combine parts of two drawings for the total score. If, for example, the first drawing contains arms but no trunk, and the second one trunk but no arms, it is incorrect to credit both arms and trunk unless both appear in one drawing.

6. Erasures should always be noted. If much erasing has been done, it is probable that the child has not been correctly rated by the test and that the true mental age is higher than that indicated by the drawing. This is especially true of older children, who have reached a stage of mental development at which they regard their work with a more critical eye. Other things being equal, erasing is always a favorable sign, even though the effect may be quite detrimental to the good appearance of the drawing.

RULES FOR SCORING

Class A

In drawings of this class the subject cannot be recognized. The total possible score is either 0 or 1. If the drawing consists merely of aimless, uncontrolled scribbling (Fig. 1), the score is 0. If the lines are somewhat controlled and appear to have been guided by the child to some extent, the score is 1. Drawings of this type most frequently take the form of a rough square, triangle, or circle, very crudely done. Not infrequently several of these forms are included in a single drawing (Fig. 2). If a drawing of this kind contains much detail, it is always well to call upon the child for an explanation, since occasionally it will be found that such a drawing belongs in Class B, rather than in Class A. Figure 3 is an example.

In questioning a child about his drawing, great care must be taken to avoid suggesting the expected answer. Be sure that his confidence has been gained before asking any direct questions. Then, after praising his drawing, say, " Now tell me about your picture. What are all these things you have made? " If this does not elicit a response, point to one of the items and say in an encouraging tone, " What is this? " If he is still unable to respond, or if, as is frequently the case, he calls each part in turn " a man," then the drawing should be scored as Class A ; but if, on the other hand, he names the various parts in a logical fashion, it should be scored according to the rules given for Class B.

Class B

This class includes all drawings which can be recognized as attempts to represent the human figure, no matter how crude they may be. Each point is scored plus or minus. A credit of 1 is allowed for each point scored plus, and no half credits are given.

1. *Head present.*

Requirement : Any clear method of representing the head. Features alone, as in Figure 4, without any outline for the head itself, are not credited for this point.

2. *Legs present.*

Requirement : Any method of representation clearly intended to indicate the legs. The number must be correct ; two in full-face drawings, either one or two in profiles.

It is always necessary to mingle a reasonable amount of common sense with what would otherwise be purely arbitrary scoring. One or two examples have been found in which only one leg was present, but a rude sketch of a crutch was included, showing clearly what the child had in mind. A more sophisticated drawing of this kind would probably show the stump of the missing leg, but it is hardly fair to expect this from a young child. On the other hand, little children sometimes draw three or more legs, or a single leg without logical explanation. These should be scored minus. A less usual occurrence is the showing of a single leg to which two feet are attached. These are scored plus.

3. *Arms present.*

Requirement : Any method of representation clearly intended to indicate arms. Fingers alone are not sufficient, but the point is credited if there is any space left between the base of the fingers and that part of the body to which they are attached. The number must also be correct. See rules for preceding point.

The only real danger of incorrect scoring of this point arises from the many remarkable methods by which the arms are indicated, and the unusual points of attachment, which makes it very easy for the beginner to overlook them. Figures 9–12 are instances of this sort.

4 a. *Trunk present.*

Requirement: Any clear indication of the trunk, whether it be by means of a straight line only (in which case, 4 *b*, it should be noted, is always minus) or by some sort of two-dimensional figure. In cases where there is no clear differentiation between the head and the trunk, but the features appear in the upper end of a single figure, the point is scored plus if the features do not occupy more than half the length of the figure; otherwise the score is minus, unless a cross line has been drawn to indicate the termination of the head. A single figure placed between the head and the legs is always counted as a trunk, even though its size and shape may be such as to suggest to the adult a neck rather than a trunk. This ruling is based on the responses of a number of children whose drawings showed this peculiarity, practically all of whom have, when questioned, called the item a trunk. A row of buttons extending down between the legs is scored minus for trunk but plus for clothing, unless a cross line has been drawn to show the termination of the trunk.

4 b. *Length of trunk greater than breadth.*

Requirement: Measurement should be taken at the points of greatest length and of greatest breadth. If the two measurements are equal, or so nearly so that the difference is not readily determined by the use of a millimeter rule, the score is minus. In most instances the difference will be found great enough to be recognized at a glance, without actually measuring. Unless the trunk is shown in two dimensions, the score is minus.

4 c. *Shoulders definitely indicated.*

Requirement: In full-face drawings, a change in the direction of the outline of the upper part of the trunk which gives an effect of concavity rather than convexity. See Figure 5. The point is scored rather strictly. The ordinary elliptical form is never credited, and the score is always minus unless it is evident that there has been a recognition of the abrupt broadening out of the trunk below the neck which is produced by the shoulder blade and the collar bone. A perfectly square or rectangular trunk does not score, but if the corners have been rounded as in Figure 6, the point is credited. (Figure 6 represents the lowest limit for which credit may be allowed.)

In profile drawings the scoring should be somewhat more lenient than in full-face drawings, since the difficulty of representing the shoulders in an adequate fashion is somewhat greater in the profile position. A profile drawing, in this connection, should be understood to mean one in which the trunk, as well as the head, is shown in profile. If the lines forming the outline of the upper part of the trunk diverge from each other at the base of the neck in such a way as to show the expansion of the chest, the point is credited.

5 a. *Attachment of arms and legs.*

Requirement: Both arms and legs attached to the trunk at any point, or arms attached to the neck, or at the junction of the head and the trunk when the neck is omitted. If the trunk is omitted, the score is always zero. If the legs are attached elsewhere than to the trunk, regardless of the attachment of the arms, the score is zero. If one arm or leg has been omitted, either in full-face or in profile drawings, credit may be given on the basis of the limb that is shown; but if both arms and legs are shown, and one is attached elsewhere than to the trunk, the score is zero. Arms attached to the legs score zero.

5 b. Legs attached to the trunk. Arms attached to the trunk at the correct point.

Requirement: In full-face drawings where 4 c is plus, the point of attachment must be exactly at the shoulders. If 4 c is minus, the attachment must be exactly at the point which should have been indicated as the shoulders. Score very strictly, especially in those cases where 4 c is minus.

In profile drawings the attachment must be indicated at a point approximately on the median line of the side trunk, at a short distance below the neck, this point coinciding with the broadening of the trunk which indicates the chest and shoulders. If, as is frequently the case, the arms extend from the line which outlines the back, or if the point of attachment reaches the base of the neck, or falls below the greatest expansion of the chest line, the point is not credited. See 5 a for ruling as to omitted limbs or misplacement of a single limb.

While this point and point 4 c tend to go together, — that is, one is more likely to be credited if the other is also credited, — this agreement is not absolute, and 5 b is more likely to be credited than is 4 c. However, success with 4 c does not insure success with 5 b, and care must be taken to differentiate between the two. It should be noted that 4 c has to do only with the shape of the upper portion of the trunk, 5 b with the point of attachment of the limbs. If this distinction is kept in mind, there should be no difficulty in scoring the two points independently of each other.

6 a. *Neck present.*

Requirement: Any clear indication of the neck as distinct from the head and the trunk. Mere juxtaposition of the head and the trunk is not credited.

6 b. *Outline of neck continuous with that of the head, of the trunk, or of both.*

See Figures 6 and 7 for examples of success with this point. There is practically never any question as to scoring.

7 a. *Eyes present.*

Requirement: Either one or two eyes must be shown. Any method is satisfactory. A single indefinite feature such as is occasionally found in the drawings of very little children is given credit here, even though its significance is uncertain.

In one of the earliest revisions of the scale, the rather obvious requirement of two eyes in full-face drawings and one in profile drawings was taken as the basis for scoring. It was found, however, that erroneous results were introduced by this method, owing to the confusion which many children undergo at the time of change from the full face to the profile. Holding to the strictly correct numerical requirement means that, in many cases, a child who for several years has been succeeding with this point in his full-face drawings suddenly begins to fail with it, not because he is any less certain of the correct number of eyes, but merely because he has not learned how to express this fact when drawing the figure from another angle.

7 b. *Nose present.*

Requirement: Any clear method of representation. In " mixed profiles " the score is plus even though two noses are shown.

In cases where only one feature has been shown in addition to the eyes, it is sometimes impossible to tell whether this feature has been intended for a nose or for a mouth. Since the child's score will be the same in either case, it does not greatly matter which way the point is credited. However, the percentages given for this and for the following point are for this reason subject to a slight degree of error.

7 c. *Mouth present.*

Requirement: Same as for the preceding point.

7 d. *Both nose and mouth shown in two dimensions; two lips shown.*

Requirement: See Figure 8 for accepted forms. In the full-face drawing any two-dimensional figure which approximates the true shape of the nose is accepted. A rough equilateral triangle is credited if in the normal position with the base downward, but not credited if the position is reversed so that it rests upon its apex. A straight line only, a dot, a circle, or a square are failures. Two dots representing the nostrils is failure here but credited for the next point.

In the full-face drawing, the mouth is credited if it is drawn in two dimensions and if the line showing the *separation* of the two lips is indicated. In practical scoring this is the point to be looked for first, as it is the one which most frequently determines success or failure. Both nose and mouth must conform to requirements if the point is to be credited.

In the profile drawing, the nose must show a clean differentiation both from the forehead and from the upper lip. The mouth must show either a separate modeling of the two lips, or the line indicating the mouth must be continuous with that outlining the remainder of the face. In very small drawings a reading glass or small magnifying glass is sometimes convenient in determining the scoring of this point, but its use is very rarely necessary. The profile drawing is very much more likely to receive credit than is the full-face drawing.

7 e. *Nostrils shown.*

Requirement: Any clear method of indicating the nostrils. In profile drawings the point is credited if the line outlining the nose is extended inward upon the upper lip as in Figure 18. A complete showing of the division of the septum (Fig. 11) is not credited. If the only indication of the nose consists of two dots representing the nostrils, the score is plus for this point and also for 7 *b*, but is minus for 7 *d*.

8 a. *Hair shown.*

Requirement: Any method clearly intended to represent hair is credited.

In scoring kindergarten drawings it is sometimes hard to distinguish between hair, hat, and fingers. The following notes will be found helpful.

In a drawing which shows no other indication of arms or fingers, but in which there appear a number of straight lines projecting from either side of the head, fingers have almost invariably been intended. See Figures 16–17.

A scribbled line on the top of the head usually represents hair.

The hat can, as a rule, be distinguished by its brim. It must not be forgotten, however, that the hair in these primitive drawings is usually visible through the hat, and any unusual shading or apparent decoration on or about the hat should be observed carefully and its relation to the outline of the head noted. If it appears to follow this outline rather than that of the hat, it is most probable that hair has been intended.

8 *b*. *Hair present on more than the circumference of the head. Better than a scribble.   Non-transparent; that is, outline of head not showing through the hair.*

Figures 18, 19, and 20 are examples of success, and Figures 21 and 22 of failure, with this point.   All three requirements must be met if the point is to be credited.

9 *a*. *Clothing present.*

Requirement: Any clear representation of clothing.   As a rule the earliest forms consist of a row of buttons running down the center of the trunk, or of a hat (which is likely to be placed above rather than on the head), or of both.   A single dot or small circle placed in the center of the trunk is practically always intended to represent the navel and should not be credited as clothing.   A series of vertical or horizontal lines drawn across the trunk — more rarely on the limbs as well — is a fairly common way of indicating striped material, and should be credited as clothing.

9 *b*. *At least two articles of clothing (as hat and trousers) non-transparent; that is, concealing the part of the body which they are supposed to cover.*

In scoring this point it must be noted that a hat which is merely in contact with the top of the head but does not cover any part of it is not credited.   Buttons alone, without any other indication of the coat, are not credited here.

9 *c*. *Entire drawing free from transparencies of any sort. Both sleeves and trousers must be shown.*

There is usually no difficulty in scoring.   In children's drawings the sleeves do not appear until a relatively late period of development — as a rule, from two to three years after the trousers are first shown.   The point is therefore a difficult one, but the correlation with school success is unusually good. 36 per cent of the accelerated nine-year-olds succeed with it, but only 7 per cent of the average and none of the retarded group of the same age do so.

9 d. *At least four articles of clothing definitely indicated.*

The articles should be among those in the following list: Hat, shoes, coat, shirt, collar, necktie, belt or suspenders, trousers.

NOTE. Shoes must show some detail, as laces, toe cap, or double line for the sole. Heel alone is not sufficient. Coat or shirt must show either sleeves, pockets, lapels, or distinctive shading, as spots or stripes. Buttons alone are not sufficient. Collar should not be confused with neck shown merely as insert, nor should coat lapels be counted as collar. The necktie is often inconspicuous and care must be taken not to overlook it, but it is not likely to be mistaken for anything else.

9 e. *Costume complete without incongruities.*

Requirement: A definite and recognizable *kind* of costume, as a business suit, a soldier's uniform, etc. Whatever the costume, it must be complete in all the essential details and there must be no confusion of any of the items, such as a sailor's hat with a business suit, etc. The scoring should be strict. The following rules should be observed as to the number of required items:

1. The *hat* must always be shown if it forms an essential part of the costume, as in the case of a uniform. It need not be shown with a business suit.

2. The *sleeves* must always be shown. Either a *coat*, as indicated by pockets, etc., must be shown or *an acceptable substitute* therefor, such as a sports shirt (with the remainder of the costume corresponding) must be present. Both *collar* and *necktie* must be shown when these would ordinarily form a part of the costume.

3. The *trousers* must always be shown.

4. The *shoes* must always be shown. See note under 9 *d*.
The only real danger of incorrect scoring of this point lies in the tendency to give credit for a large number of unimportant or non-essential details in spite of the absence of essentials. This is especially likely to be the case in the drawings representing " cowboys " and " Indians," two subjects which are extremely popular with retarded boys of nine to twelve years. One frequently finds in these drawings a great amount of detail — elaborately drawn " chaps," cartridge belts, revolvers, etc., but no sleeves. (Fringes on the arms similar to those on the trousers may not be counted as sleeves unless the cross line at the wrist, showing the termination of the sleeve, is present.)

10 *a*. *Fingers present*.

Requirement: Any clear indication of fingers, no matter what may be the method of representation. They must be shown on both hands if both hands are present, but credit is given for fingers on one hand if only one hand is shown.

NOTE. Little children sometimes express the fingers in very curious ways, and the scorer must be on his guard to avoid overlooking such cases. A number of these bizarre types are shown in Figures 13–17. Sully (*115*) has described in detail the various methods of picturing the hand and fingers which were found in his collection, and a study of his article in this connection is well worth while. See also the note on 8 *a* which calls attention to the likelihood of confusing fingers and hair.

10 *b*. *Correct number of fingers shown*.

Requirement: Five fingers on each hand where both hands are shown ; on one hand if only one hand is shown. In cases where both hands are shown but one is partially concealed, as in carrying something, credit may be given on the basis of the one hand that is entirely visible, if there is no question regarding the number of fingers on that hand and the concealment of fingers on the other hand is logically demanded by the situation. This ruling must be interpreted very rigidly, however, and credit allowed only in cases in which the above conditions are unquestionably applicable.

10 *c*. *Detail of fingers correct.*

Requirement: Fingers must be shown in two dimensions, the length in all cases must be greater than the breadth, and the angle subtended by them must not be greater than 180 degrees. As in the preceding point, if one hand is not shown, credit is given on the basis of the hand that is present. All three requirements must be fulfilled if the point is to be credited.

10 *d*. *Opposition of thumb shown.*

Requirement: A clear differentiation of the thumb from the fingers. Scoring should be very strict. The point is credited if one of the lateral digits is definitely shorter than any of the others — compare especially with the little finger — or if the angle between it and the index finger is not less than twice as great as that between any two of the other digits, or if its point of attachment to the hand is distinctly nearer to the wrist than that of the fingers. Conditions must be fulfilled on both hands if both are shown; one hand is sufficient if only one is shown.

10 *e*. *Hand shown as distinct from fingers or arm.*

See Figures 23–27 for some of the most common ways of picturing the hand. There is usually no difficulty in scoring.

A small percentage, usually of the brighter children, who have come to realize the technical difficulties involved in drawing the hands, avoid the issue by concealing them in some way, usually by drawing the man with his hands in his pockets. In these cases the child should be credited with points 10 *a*, 10 *b*, and 10 *c*; not with 10 *d*, and with 10 *e* only in case the upper part of the hand is visible above the pockets. This ruling is based upon the average score made on the remainder of the drawing by children who drew the hands in this position.

11 *a*. *Arm joint shown. Either elbow, shoulder, or both.*

Requirement: If the elbow joint is taken as the basis for scoring, there must be an abrupt *bend* (not a curve) at approximately the middle of the arm. One arm is sufficient in this case. If the shoulder joint is taken, the arm must hang at the side *in a position approximately parallel to the body axis.* An arm which simply points in a downward direction does not score; there must be a curve at the point of attachment to the body, to indicate the shoulder joint. While this point is more likely to be gained if 4 *c* and 5 *b* are also credited, yet success with any one of them does not necessarily mean success with either of the others. For the sake of clearness, the distinction between these points is repeated here:

4 *c* depends upon the shape of the upper portion of the trunk.

5 *b* depends upon the *point* of attachment of the arms.

11 *a* depends upon the *manner* of attaching the arms, and the angle between the arms and the body axis.

Drawings are occasionally found in which the arm does not hang at the side; yet 11 *a* should obviously be credited since there is a clear indication of the shoulder joint, as when the man is reaching out to get something. Because of the marked tendency of little children to draw the arms standing stiffly out from the side, it is necessary to exercise great caution in giving credit for this point unless at least one arm hangs at the side. Both arms must do so if both are shown, unless there is a logical reason for the change in position. See Figures 28–31. Note that in Figure 28, 11 *a* is credited although both 4 *c* and 5 *b* are failures. Compare this drawing with Figure 23, which represents the upper limit of failure in point 11 *a*. In Figure 23 the curve was determined in part by the size of the sheet of paper.

In drawings made by young or backward children, the position of the elbows and knees is sometimes indicated, without apparent recognition of their function as joints. See Figures 33–34. No credit is allowed for joints in these cases. (In Figure 34 credit has been given for the hip joint.)

11 *b*. *Leg joint shown. Either knee, hip, or both.*

Requirement: If the knee joint is taken as a basis for scoring, there must be, as in the case of the elbow, an abrupt *bend* at about the middle of the leg, or, as is sometimes found in very high-grade drawings, a narrowing of the leg at this point. Knee-length trousers are not sufficient. The hip joint is the one most frequently shown. If the inner lines of the two legs meet at the point of junction with the body, the point is credited. Young children usually place the legs as far apart from each other as possible.

12 *a*. *Proportion. Head.*

Requirement: Area of the head not more than one half or less than one tenth that of the trunk. Score rather leniently. See Figure 32 for a series of standard forms of which the first is double the area of the second.

12 *b*. *Proportion. Arms.*

Requirement: Arms equal to the trunk in length or slightly longer, but in no case reaching to the knee. Width of arms less than that of trunk.

12 *c*. *Proportion. Legs.*

Requirement: Length of the legs not less than the vertical measurement of the trunk, nor greater than twice that measurement. Width of the legs less than that of the trunk.

12 d. Proportion. Feet.

Requirement: The feet and legs must be shown in two dimensions. The feet must not be " clubbed "; that is, the length of the foot must be greater than its height from sole to instep. The length of the foot must be not more than one third or less than one tenth the total length of the leg. The point is also credited in full-face drawings in which the foot is shown in perspective, as in Figure 35, *provided* that the foot is separated in some way from the rest of the leg in these drawings.

12 e. Proportion. Two dimensions.

Requirement: Both arms and legs shown in two dimensions. If the arms and legs are in two dimensions, the point is credited even though the hands and feet are in linear dimension only.

13. Heel shown.

Requirement: Any clear method of indicating the heel. See Figures 36–38 for the method most frequently found. The point is also credited in full-face drawings where the foot is shown in perspective, as in Figure 35.

14 a. Motor coördination. Lines A.

Requirement: All lines reasonably firm, for the most part meeting each other cleanly at points of junction, without marked tendency to cross or overlap, or to leave gaps between the ends. The degree of complexity of the drawing must be taken into account, a drawing with very few lines being scored more rigidly than one which involves much detail and frequent change in the direction of the lines. A " sketchy " drawing in which most of the outlines consist of many short lines is ordinarily credited, since this is a characteristic confined almost entirely to drawings of a rather mature type.

For the scoring of this and the other five points in this group, reference should be made to the series of specimen drawings on pages 112–161. While the scoring of these points is perhaps slightly less objective than that of most of the others in the scale, a study of the types presented should produce results which are at least as consistent as those obtained by the ordinary handwriting scale, in which essentially the same method of comparison is used.

14 b. *Motor coördination. Lines B.*

Requirement: All lines firmly drawn with correct joining.

This point is based upon a much more rigid interpretation of the rules given for the scoring of the preceding point. Obviously it can never be credited unless 14 *a* is also credited. The score is in addition to that for 14 *a*. Scoring should be very strict.

14 c. *Motor coördination. Head outline.*

Requirement: Outline of head without obviously unintentional irregularities. The point is credited only in those drawings in which the shape of the head has developed beyond the first crude circle or ellipse, so that conscious control of the movement of the hand is necessary throughout. Scoring should be rather strict.

14 d. *Motor coördination. Trunk outline.*

Requirement: Same as for the preceding point, but here with reference to the trunk. Note that the primitive circle or ellipse does not score.

14 e. *Motor coördination. Arms and legs.*

Requirement: Arms and legs without irregularities as above, and without tendency to narrowing at the point of junction with the body. Both arms and legs must be in two dimensions.

14 f. *Motor coördination. Features.*

Requirement: Features symmetrical in all respects. Eyes, nose, and mouth must all be shown in two dimensions. In full-face drawings the eyes must be equidistant from the nose and from the corners of the mouth, and there must be no incorrect juxtaposition with the outline of the head. The nose must be symmetrical in shape, and must be placed above the center of the mouth. Where the nose is represented by two dots, these must be equidistant from the corners of the mouth. The two sides of the mouth must be alike, and the mouth must be placed at right angles with the axis of the head. In profile drawings the eye must be regular in outline and the distance from the center of the eye to the back of the head must be not less than twice as great as the distance from the center of the eye measured forward to the edge of the nose. The nose must form an obtuse angle with the forehead, and its size must be in proportion to the other features and to the size of the head. The mouth must be regular in outline and of a size proportionate to the other features. The scoring should be strict.

The point is much more likely to be credited in profile drawings than in full-face drawings.

15 a. *Ears present.*

Requirement: Two in full-face drawings, one in profile. Any clear method of representation.

Care must be taken not to overlook inconspicuous or unusual methods of showing the ears. Figures 43–46 show some of the bizarre forms under which this item may appear. In some kindergarten drawings there is danger of confusing ears and arms. It should be remembered that, as a rule, the arms are shown at an earlier age than the ears; hence in cases of doubt it is usually safer to call the unexplained feature an arm rather than an ear, unless the size and shape are such as to make the classification fairly certain. As a rule the total rating of the child will not be affected whichever way the point is credited, since a score of more than one point on either item is not usual in these primitive drawings.

15 *b*. *Ears present in correct position and proportion*.

Requirement: The vertical measurement must be greater than the horizontal measurement. In profile drawings some detail, such as a dot to represent the aural canal, must be shown. In full-face drawings such detail may or may not be present. The ears must be placed somewhere within the middle two thirds of the head (as viewed from the side) and the shell-like portion of the ear must extend toward the back of the head. For some unexplained reason, a fairly large number of children, especially of retarded boys, tend to reverse this position, making the ear extend toward the face (Fig. 46). In such drawings point 15 *b* is never credited.

16 *a*. *Eye detail. Brow, lashes, or both shown*.

Requirement: Any clear method of representation. In most instances the brow is shown by means of a curved line above the eye. In some profile drawings of a high grade it is indicated by modeling to show the supraorbital ridge. Either method is satisfactory. Lashes are almost invariably represented by means of a series of curved lines projecting from the outline of the eye.

16 *b*. *Eye detail. Pupil shown*.

There is rarely any question as to the scoring. It should be noted, however, that a dot with a curved line above it is not credited, since the dot must be considered as representing the eye itself in these cases. The pupil must be present in both eyes if both are shown.

16 c. *Eye detail. Proportion.*

Requirement: The horizontal measurement of the eye must be greater than the vertical measurement. This requirement must be fulfilled in both eyes if both are shown; one eye is sufficient if only one is shown. In profile drawings of a high grade, the eye is sometimes shown in perspective; that is, its shape is altered from the customary almond form to that of a sector of a circle. In all such cases the point should be credited.

16 d. *Eye detail. Glance.*

Requirement: The face must be shown in profile. The eye must either be shown in perspective, as described in the preceding paragraph, or, if the ordinary almond form is retained, the pupil must be placed toward the front of the eye rather than in the center. The scoring should be strict.

17 a. *Both chin and forehead shown.*

In full-face drawings both the eyes and the mouth must be present, and sufficient space must be left above the eyes to represent the forehead, below the mouth to represent the chin. The scoring should be rather lenient. In profile drawings the point may also be credited when the eyes and mouth are omitted, if the outline of the face shows clearly the limits of the chin and forehead. If there is no outline to indicate the separation of the chin from the neck in full-face drawings, the point cannot be credited. See Figures 47–50 for examples of success and failure. Note also the unusual methods of showing the chin and forehead, in Figures 51–54.

The reliability of scoring is rather less for this point than for most others in the scale. A number of scoring methods have been tried in an attempt to devise a purely objective rule for determining what is to be considered " sufficient " space. Comparative vertical measurements of different kinds, and combinations of vertical and horizontal measurements, using as a basis the total size of the head, the distance from the eyes to the top of the head, distance from the eyes to the mouth, etc., were tried; but no simple standard could be devised which would make sufficient allowance for the great variations in the shape of the head and in the relationships of the several features to each other. Because of this difficulty in scoring, the point was entirely omitted from one of the earlier forms of the scale. It was re-included in the present revision because of its apparent significance in the case of kindergarten and first-grade children. There is little difference between the performance of accelerated and average children in respect to this point, but the retarded group is clearly behind the others at all age levels.

17 b. *Projection of chin shown; chin clearly differentiated from lower lip.*

The point is rarely credited except in profile drawings. In full-face drawings, however, it may be credited if the modeling of the chin is indicated in some way, as by a curved line below the lip.

18 a. *Profile A.*

Requirement: The head, trunk, and feet must be shown in profile without error. The trunk may not be considered as drawn in profile unless the characteristic line of buttons has been moved from the center to the side of the figure, or some other indication, such as the position of the arms, pockets, necktie, etc., shows clearly the effect of this change of position. The entire drawing may contain one, but not more than one, of the following errors:

1. One bodily transparency, as the outline of the trunk showing through the arm.

2. Legs not in profile. In a true profile at least the upper

part of the leg which is in the background must be concealed by the one in the foreground.

3. Arms attached to the outline of the back and extending forward. This appears to be a residual effect of the manner of attachment which the child was accustomed to use in his full-face drawings.

18 b. *Profile B.*

Requirement: The figure must be shown in true profile, without error or bodily transparency, except that the shape of the eye may be ignored.

Considering the strong emphasis which previous workers have placed upon the change from the full-face to the profile drawing, it may seem that too little weight has been given to this characteristic in the present scale. It has been found, however, that while it is true that very young children practically never draw the figure in profile, an appreciable number of older ones, even among the accelerated children, continue to give the preference to the full-face position. Most of the literature on children's drawings tends to give the impression that the change to the profile position is a general rule which all children come to adopt in their drawings, but my own figures show that this is far from being the case. The proportion of profiles, when the subject is left entirely to his own choice, increases steadily until it includes about 80 or 85 per cent of all drawings; but apparently the maximum is reached at about this point. At least this is the approximate proportion found among drawings by high school students and university graduates. It has therefore seemed best not to give too much credit to the profile as such; rather, to devise a scoring plan which would tend to favor the profile position in a large number of the points considered, but which would not preclude the possibility of success with these points in the full-face drawing.

CHAPTER SEVEN

Specimen Drawings, with Scoring Indicated

Series I

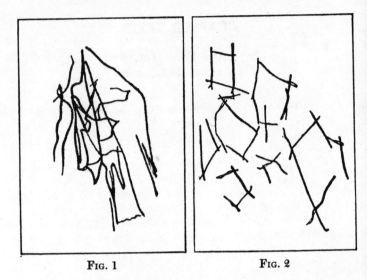

FIG. 1   FIG. 2

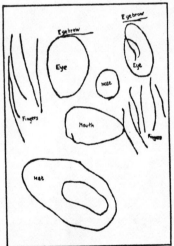

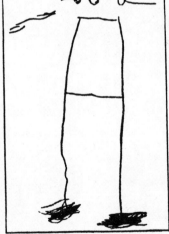

FIG. 3   FIG. 4

Fig. 1. Boy, Italian, age 4–2, pre-school. Score 0. (Class A.) M.A. not over 3 years. IQ 72 or less.

Fig. 2. Girl, American, age 4–2, kindergarten. Score 1. (Class A.) M.A. 3–3. IQ 78.

Fig. 3. Boy, Jewish, age 4–11, kindergarten. Credits, 7 a, 7 b, 7 c, 9 a, 10 a, 16 a. Total score 6. M.A. 4–6. IQ 92. (This and all subsequent drawings belong to Class B.)

Fig. 4. Girl, American, age 5–0, kindergarten. Credits, 2, 3, 4 a, 4 b, 7 a, 7 b, 12 c. Total score 7. M.A. 4–9. IQ 95.

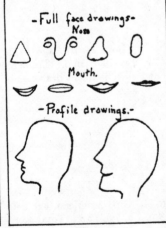

FIG. 5

FIG. 6

FIG. 7

FIG. 8

FIG. 5. Girl, American, age 11–7, high third grade. Credits, 1, 2, 3, 4 *a*, 4 *b*, 4 *c*, 5 *a*, 5 *b*, 7 *a*, 7 *b*, 7 *c*, 7 *e*, 9 *a*, 9 *b*, 9 *d*, 10 *a*, 10 *c*, 10 *e*, 11 *a*, 11 *b*, 12 *a*, 12 *e*, 14 *a*, 14 *d*, 17 *a*. Total score 25. M.A. 9–3. IQ 80.

FIG. 6. Boy, Negro, age 10–1, low third grade. Credits, 1, 2, 3, 4 *a*, 4 *c*, 5 *a*, 5 *b*, 6 *a*, 6 *b*, 7 *a*, 7 *b*, 7 *c*, 7 *e*, 8 *a*, 8 *b*, 9 *a*, 9 *b*, 9 *c*, 9 *d*, 10 *a*, 10 *c*, 12 *a*, 12 *c*, 12 *d*, 12 *e*, 13, 14 *a*, 14 *c*, 14 *f*, 16 *a*, 17 *a*. Total score 31. M.A. 10–9. IQ 107.

FIG. 7. Girl, Indian, age 12–3, fourth grade. Credits, 1, 2, 3, 4 *a*, 4 *b*, 4 *c*, 5 *a*, 5 *b*, 6 *a*, 6 *b*, 7 *a*, 7 *b*, 7 *c*, 7 *e*, 8 *a*, 8 *b*,[1] 9 *a*, 9 *b*, 9 *c*, 9 *d*, 10 *a*, 10 *b*, 10 *c*, 10 *d*, 10 *e*, 11 *a*, 11 *b*, 12 *b*, 12 *c*, 12 *d*, 12 *e*, 13, 14 *a*, 14 *d*, 14 *e*, 15 *a*, 15 *b*, 16 *b*, 16 *c*. Total score 39. M.A. 12–9. IQ 104.

FIG. 8. Accepted forms for scoring point 7 *d*.

[1] In drawings of the type of Figure 7, in which practically all of the hair is covered by the hat, credit is given for point 8 *b* if the hair which is shown covers even a very small portion of the visible part of the head.

Fig. 9

Fig. 10

Fig. 11

Fig. 12

Fig. 9. Girl, American, age 5–7, kindergarten. Credits, 1, 2, 3, 4 *a*, 4 *b*, 7 *a*, 7 *b*, 15 *a*. Total score 8. M.A. 5–0. IQ 90.

Fig. 10. Girl, German, age 7–6, high first grade. Credits, 1, 2, 3, 4 *a*, 5 *a*, 6 *a*, 7 *a*, 7 *b*, 7 *c*, 7 *d*, 8 *a*, 9 *a*, 12 *e*, 14 *a*, 16 *a*, 16 *c*. Total score 16. M.A. 7–0. IQ 93.

Fig. 11. Girl, American, age 5–10, kindergarten. Credits, 1, 2, 3, 7 *a*, 7 *b*, 7 *c*, 16 *a*. Total score 7. M.A. 4–9. IQ 81. (Note the division of the septum. This is not credited as nostrils.)

Fig. 12. Boy, Jewish, age 8–11, low second grade. Credits, 1, 2, 3, 4 *a*, 4 *b*, 5 *a*, 7 *a*, 7 *b*, 7 *c*, 8 *a*, 9 *a*, 10 *e*, 15 *a*, 16 *b*. Total score 14. M.A. 6–6. IQ 73.

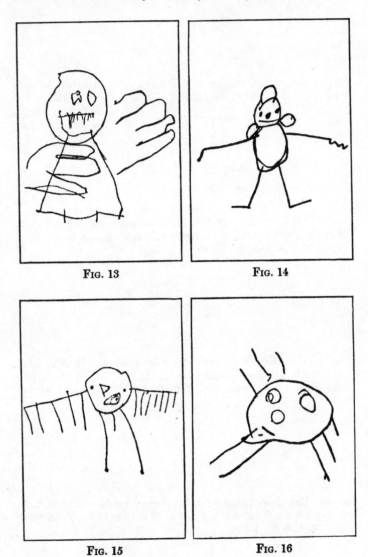

FIG. 13   FIG. 14

FIG. 15   FIG. 16

FIG. 13. Boy, American, age 4–7, kindergarten. Credits, 1, 2, 3, 4 *a*, 5 *a*, 7 *a*, 7 *c*, 10 *a*, 10 *c*, 17 *a*. Total score 10. M.A. 5–6. IQ 120.

FIG. 14. Boy, American, age 5–10, kindergarten. Credits, 1, 2, 3, 4 *a*, 4 *b*, 5 *a*, 7 *a*, 7 *b*, 7 *c*, 9 *a*, 10 *a*, 12 *a*, 12 *c*, 15 *a*, 17 *a*. Total score 15. M.A. 6–9. IQ 116.

FIG. 15. Girl, American, age 5–6, kindergarten. Credits, 1, 2, 3, 7 *a*, 7 *b*, 7 *c*, 10 *a*, 17 *a*. Total score 8. M.A. 5–0. IQ 91.

FIG. 16. Girl, Italian, age 6–0, pre-school. Credits, 1, 2, 7 *a*, 7 *b*, 7 *c*, 10 *a*. Total score 6. M.A. 4–6. IQ 75.

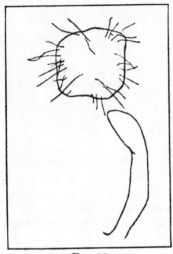

Fig. 17

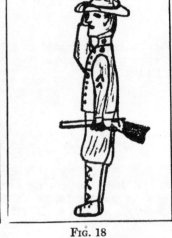

Fig. 18

Fig. 19

Fig. 20

FIG. 17. Boy, Jewish, age 4–0, pre-school. Credits, 1, 2, 10 *a*. Total score 3. M.A. 3–9. IQ 94.

FIG. 18. Boy, Jewish, age 12–9, high fourth grade. Credits, 1, 2, 3, 4 *a*, 4 *b*, 4 *c*, 5 *a*, 5 *b*, 6 *a*, 6 *b*, 7 *a*, 7 *b*, 7 *c*, 7 *d*, 7 *e*, 8 *a*, 8 *b*, 9 *a*, 9 *b*, 9 *c*, 9 *d*, 9 *e*, 10 *a*, 10 *b*, 10 *c*, 10 *e*, 11 *a*, 11 *b*, 12 *a*, 12 *b*, 12 *c*, 12 *d*, 12 *e*, 13, 14 *a*, 14 *c*, 14 *d*, 14 *e*, 14 *f*, 15 *a*, 16 *b*, 16 *c*, 17 *a*, 17 *b*, 18 *a*, 18 *b*. Total score 46. M.A. 13–0 or above. IQ 102 or above.

FIG. 19. Girl, Negro, age 12–3, high third grade. Credits, 1, 2, 3, 4 *a*, 4 *b*, 5 *a*, 6 *a*, 6 *b*, 7 *a*, 7 *b*, 7 *c*, 8 *a*, 8 *b*, 9 *a*, 9 *b*, 9 *d*, 10 *a*, 10 *b*, 10 *c*, 11 *a*, 11 *b*, 12 *b*, 12 *c*, 12 *d*, 12 *e*, 13, 14 *a*, 14 *f*, 15 *a*, 15 *b*, 16 *a*, 17 *a*, 17 *b*. Total score 33. M.A. 11–3. IQ 92.

FIG. 20. Girl, Armenian, age 9–3, high third grade. Credits, 1, 2, 3, 4 *a*, 4 *b*, 4 *c*, 5 *a*, 5 *b*, 6 *a*, 6 *b*, 7 *a*, 7 *b*, 7 *c*, 7 *d*, 7 *e*, 8 *a*, 8 *b*, 9 *a*, 9 *b*, 9 *c*, 9 *d*, 9 *e*, 10 *a*, 10 *e*, 11 *a*, 11 *b*, 12 *a*, 12 *b*, 12 *c*, 12 *d*, 12 *e*, 13, 14 *a*, 14 *c*, 14 *f*, 15 *a*, 15 *b*, 16 *a*, 16 *b*, 16 *c*, 16 *d*, 17 *a*, 17 *b*, 18 *a*. Total score 44. M.A. 13–0 or above. IQ 141 or above.

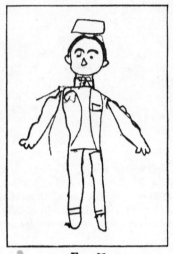

FIG. 21

FIG. 22

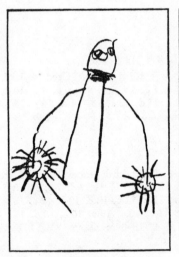

FIG. 23

FIG. 24

Fɪɢ. 21. Girl, Negro, age 12–6, high third grade.   Credits, 1, 2, 3, 4 *a*, 4 *b*, 4 *c*, 5 *a*, 5 *b*, 6 *a*, 7 *a*, 7 *b*, 8 *a*, 9 *a*, 9 *d*, 10 *a*, 12 *a*, 12 *b*, 12 *c*, 12 *d*, 12 *e*, 13, 15 *a*, 16 *a*.   Total score 23.   M.A. 8–9.   IQ 70.

Fɪɢ. 22. Girl, Jewish, age 5–9, kindergarten.   Credits, 1, 2, 3, 4 *a*, 4 *b*, 5 *a*, 7 *a*, 7 *b*, 7 *c*, 7 *e*, 8 *a*, 9 *a*, 10 *e*, 12 *a*, 12 *b*.   Total score 15.   M.A. 6–9.   IQ 117.

Fɪɢ. 23. Girl, Italian, age 4–9, kindergarten.   Credits, 1, 2, 3, 7 *a*, 7 *b*, 7 *c*, 10 *a*, 10 *e*, 16 *b*.   Total score 9.   M.A. 5–3.   IQ 112.

Fɪɢ. 24. Boy, American, age 7–11, low second grade.   Credits, 1, 2, 3, 4 *a*, 4 *b*, 5 *a*, 7 *a*, 7 *b*, 7 *c*, 7 *e*, 9 *a*, 10 *e*, 16 *a*.   Total score 13.   M.A. 6–3.   IQ 79.

FIG. 25

FIG. 26

FIG. 27

FIG. 28

FIG. 25. Boy, Italian, age 7–2, low second grade.   Credits, 1, 2, 3, 4 *a*, 4 *b*, 5 *a*, 7 *a*, 7 *b*, 7 *e*, 9 *a*, 10 *a*, 10 *b*, 10 *e*, 12 *c*, 14 *a*, 16 *b*, 16 *c*.   Total score 17.   M.A. 7–3.   IQ 101.

FIG. 26. Boy, Italian, age 7–2, low first grade.   Credits, 1, 2, 3, 7 *a*, 7 *b*, 7 *c*, 10 *a*, 10 *e*, 15 *a*.   Total score 9.   M.A. 5–3.   IQ 73.

FIG. 27. Boy, American, age 9–6, high fourth grade.   Credits, 1, 2, 3, 4 *a*, 4 *b*, 4 *c*, 5 *a*, 6 *a*, 6 *b*, 7 *a*, 7 *b*, 8 *a*, 9 *a*, 9 *b*, 9 *c*, 10 *a*, 10 *b*, 10 *c*, 10 *d*, 10 *e*, 12 *a*, 12 *c*, 12 *e*, 13, 14 *a*, 16 *a*.   Total score 26.   M.A. 9–6.   IQ 100.

FIG. 28. Boy, Polish, age 12–4, low third grade.   Credits, 1, 2, 3, 4 *a*, 4 *b*, 5 *a*, 6 *a*, 6 *b*, 7 *a*, 7 *b*, 7 *c*, 8 *a*, 9 *a*, 10 *e*, 11 *a*, 12 *d*, 12 *e*, 13, 14 *a*, 16 *a*, 17 *a*.   Total score 21.   M.A. 8–3.   IQ 67.

FIG. 29

FIG. 30

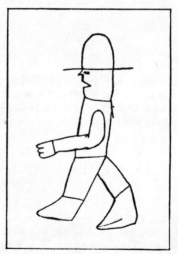

FIG. 31

FIG. 29. Boy, Negro, age 11–7, low fourth grade. Credits, 1, 2, 3, 4 *a*, 4 *b*, 4 *c*, 5 *a*, 5 *b*, 6 *a*, 6 *b*, 7 *a*, 7 *b*, 7 *c*, 7 *d*, 8 *a*, 8 *b*, 9 *a*, 9 *b*, 9 *d*, 9 *e*, 10 *a*, 10 *c*, 10 *e*, 11 *a*, 11 *b*, 12 *a*, 12 *b*, 12 *c*, 12 *d*, 12 *e*, 13, 14 *a*, 14 *d*, 14 *e*, 15 *a*, 16 *a*, 17 *a*, 18 *a*. Total score 38. M.A. 12–6. IQ 108. (NOTE. The neck is shown only in the back, owing to the pose of the head. The hair is not clear in the photograph, but is distinct in the original drawing. The thumb shown on the glove does not score, since none is shown on the other hand. The heel is shown by projection at back of foot.)

FIG. 30. Girl, American, age 9–6, high third grade. Credits, 1, 2, 3, 4 *a*, 4 *b*, 5 *a*, 5 *b*, 7 *a*, 7 *b*, 7 *c*, 7 *e*, 9 *a*, 9 *b*, 9 *d*, 10 *a*, 10 *b*, 10 *c*, 11 *a*, 11 *b*, 12 *a*, 12 *b*, 12 *d*, 12 *e*, 14 *a*, 16 *a*, 16 *c*. Total score 26. M.A. 9–6. IQ 100.

FIG. 31. Boy, Chinese, age 6–7, low first grade. Credits, 1, 2, 3, 4 *a*, 5 *a*, 5 *b*, 7 *a*, 7 *b*, 7 *c*, 7 *d*, 9 *a*, 9 *b*, 9 *c*, 10 *a*, 10 *c*, 10 *e*, 11 *a*, 11 *b*, 12 *c*, 12 *e*, 14 *a*, 16 *c*, 17 *a*, 18 *a*, 18 *b*. Total score 25. M.A. 9–3. IQ 141.

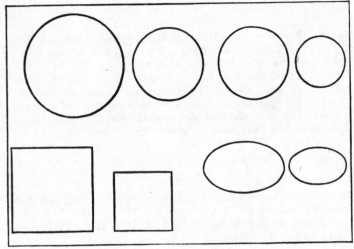

FIG. 32

FIG. 33

FIG. 34

Fɪɢ. 32. Standard forms in which the area of the second is one half of the first. For comparison in scoring point 12 *a*.

Fɪɢ. 33. Boy, American, age 6–9, low second grade. Credits, 1, 2, 3, 4 *a*, 4 *b*, 4 *c*, 5 *a*, 5 *b*, 6 *a*, 7 *a*, 7 *b*, 7 *c*, 8 *a*, 8 *b*, 10 *a*, 10 *b*, 10 *c*, 10 *e*, 12 *a*, 12 *b*, 12 *e*, 14 *a*, 14 *c*, 15 *a*. Total score 24. M.A. 9–0. IQ 133.

Fɪɢ. 34. Girl, American, age 11–8, low second grade. Credits, 1, 2, 3, 4 *a*, 4 *b*, 5 *a*, 6 *a*, 7 *a*, 9 *a*, 10 *a*, 10 *e*, 11 *a*, 11 *b*, 12 *a*, 12 *e*, 18 *a*. Total score 16. M.A. 7–0. IQ 60. (9 *a* is credited on basis of sleeve.)

FIG. 35

FIG. 36

FIG. 37

FIG. 38

Fɪɢ. 35. Girl, Scotch, age 7–0, high first grade. Credits, 1, 2, 3, 4 *a*, 5 *a*, 7 *a*, 7 *b*, 7 *c*, 7 *e*, 8 *a*, 9 *a*, 10 *a*, 10 *c*, 11 *b*, 12 *a*, 12 *c*, 12 *d*, 12 *e*, 13, 16 *a*. Total score 20. M.A. 8–0. IQ 114.

Fɪɢ. 36. Boy, Italian, age 5–7, kindergarten. Credits, 1, 2, 3, 7 *a*, 7 *c*, 10 *a*, 13. Total score 7. M.A. 4–9. IQ 85. (Note that the mouth, which can be identified by the teeth, is placed above the eyes. The smaller ellipse represents the face.)

Fɪɢ. 37. Boy, Negro, age 14–5, low third grade. Credits, 1, 2, 3, 4 *a*, 4 *c*, 5 *a*, 6 *a*, 6 *b*, 7 *a*, 7 *b*, 7 *c*, 8 *a*, 8 *b*, 9 *a*, 10 *a*, 10 *b*, 10 *c*, 10 *d*, 10 *e*, 12 *a*, 12 *b*, 12 *d*, 12 *e*, 13, 14 *a*, 14 *c*, 14 *d*, 15 *a*, 17 *a*, 17 *b*. Total score 30. M.A. 10–6. IQ 71 or less. (IQ computed on basis of chronological age of 13–0.)

Fɪɢ. 38. Boy, American, age 14–7, low second grade. Credits, 1, 2, 3, 4 *a*, 4 *b*, 7 *a*, 7 *b*, 8 *a*, 9 *a*, 10 *a*, 12 *c*, 13. Total score 12. M.A. 6–0. IQ 46. (IQ computed on basis of chronological age of 13–0.)

FIG. 39

FIG. 40

FIG. 41

FIG. 42

FIG. 39. Boy, Armenian, age 11–2, low fifth grade. Credits, 1, 2, 3, 4 *a*, 4 *b*, 4 *c*, 5 *a*, 5 *b*, 6 *a*, 6 *b*, 7 *a*, 7 *b*, 7 *c*, 7 *d*, 7 *e*, 8 *a*, 8 *b*, 9 *a*, 9 *b*, 9 *c*, 9 *d*, 9 *e*, 10 *a*, 10 *b*, 11 *a*, 11 *b*, 12 *a*, 12 *b*, 12 *c*, 12 *e*, 13, 14 *a*, 14 *b*, 14 *c*, 14 *d*, 14 *e*, 14 *f*, 15 *a*, 16 *a*, 16 *b*, 16 *c*, 16 *d*, 17 *a*, 17 *b*, 18 *a*, 18 *b*.   Total score 47.   M.A. 13–0 or above.   IQ 116 or above.

FIG. 40. Boy, Negro, age 10–4, low third grade.   Credits, 1, 2, 3, 4 *a*, 5 *a*, 6 *a*, 7 *a*, 7 *b*, 7 *c*, 9 *a*, 10 *a*, 10 *b*, 10 *c*, 11 *b*, 12 *b*, 12 *c*, 12 *d*, 12 *e*, 13, 14 *a*, 14 *c*, 14 *f*, 16 *a*, 17 *a*.   Total score 24.   M.A. 9–0.   IQ 87.   (A short inserted neck is present, not clearly shown in the photograph.)

FIG. 41. Boy, American, age 9–4, low third grade.   Credits, 1, 2, 4 *a*, 7 *a*, 7 *b*, 7 *c*, 9 *a*, 12 *c*, 12 *d*, 14 *a*, 16 *a*, 16 *b*, 17 *a*.   Total score 13.   M.A. 6–3.   IQ 67.

FIG. 42. Boy, Italian, age 7–6, high first grade.   Credits, 1, 2, 3, 4 *a*, 4 *b*, 7 *a*, 7 *b*, 7 *c*, 9 *a*, 10 *a*, 10 *b*.   Total score 11.   M.A. 5–9.   IQ 77.

FIG. 43

FIG. 44

FIG. 45

FIG. 46

Fɪɢ. 43. Boy, Italian, age 5–3, kindergarten. Credits, 1, 2, 3, 4 *a*, 5 *a*, 7 *a*, 7 *b*, 7 *c*, 8 *a*, 9 *a*, 10 *a*, 10 *e*, 12 *b*, 15 *a*. Total score 14. M.A. 6–6. IQ 124. (One ear is attached to the head; the other to the arm on the opposite side. The line around the head signifies the hat. Trousers' pockets but no trousers are shown. The scribbled line inside the mouth is the tongue.)

Fɪɢ. 44. Girl, Negro, age 9–9, low third grade. Credits, 1, 2, 3, 4 *a*, 5 *a*, 6 *a*, 6 *b*, 7 *a*, 7 *b*, 7 *c*, 7 *e*, 9 *a*, 10 *a*, 10 *e*, 12 *d*, 12 *e*, 14 *a*, 15 *a*, 16 *a*. Total score 19. M.A. 7–9. IQ 79.

Fɪɢ. 45. Girl, Japanese, age 4–10, kindergarten. Credits, 1, 2, 4 *a*, 4 *b*, 7 *a*, 7 *b*, 7 *c*, 7 *e*, 9 *a*, 12 *c*, 15 *a*, 16 *a*, 17 *a*. Total score 13. M.A. 6–3. IQ 129.

Fɪɢ. 46. Boy, American, age 11–5, low fifth grade. Credits, 1, 2, 3, 4 *a*, 4 *b*, 5 *a*, 5 *b*, 6 *a*, 6 *b*, 7 *a*, 7 *b*, 7 *c*, 7 *d*, 9 *a*, 9 *b*, 9 *c*, 9 *d*, 10 *a*, 10 *c*, 11 *a*, 11 *b*, 12 *a*, 12 *e*, 13, 14 *a*, 14 *c*, 14 *f*, 15 *a*, 16 *b*, 16 *c*, 17 *a*, 17 *b*, 18 *a*. Total score 33. M.A. 11–3. IQ 99.

FIG. 47

FIG. 48

FIG. 49

FIG. 50

Fig. 47. Girl, Indian, age 12–5, fourth grade. Credits, 1, 2, 3, 4 *a*, 4 *b*, 4 *c*, 5 *a*, 5 *b*, 6 *a*, 6 *b*, 7 *a*, 7 *b*, 7 *c*, 7 *d*, 8 *a*, 8 *b*, 9 *a*, 9 *b*, 9 *d*, 10 *a*, 10 *b*, 10 *c*, 10 *d*, 10 *e*, 11 *b*, 12 *e*, 13, 14 *a*, 14 *c*, 14 *f*, 15 *a*, 16 *a*, 16 *b*, 16 *c*, 17 *a*, 17 *b*. Total score 36. M.A. 12–0. IQ 97.

Fig. 48. Girl, Finnish, age 4–11, kindergarten. Credits, 1, 2, 3, 7 *a*, 7 *b*, 7 *c*, 9 *a*, 10 *a*, 12 *e*, 16 *a*. Total score 10. M.A. 5–6. IQ 112.

Fig. 49. Boy, Jewish, age 4–11, pre-school. Credits, 1, 2, 3, 7 *a*, 7 *c*, 10 *a*, 17 *a*. Total score 7. M.A. 4–9. IQ 97. (Scribbling for eyes not an indication of pupil.)

Fig. 50. Girl, Negro, age 13–11, low fourth grade. Credits, 1, 2, 3, 4 *a*, 4 *b*, 5 *a*, 7 *a*, 7 *b*, 7 *c*, 7 *e*, 8 *a*, 8 *b*, 9 *a*, 9 *b*, 9 *c*, 9 *d*, 10 *a*, 10 *b*, 10 *c*, 11 *a*, 11 *b*, 12 *a*, 12 *b*, 12 *d*, 12 *e*, 13, 14 *a*, 14 *e*, 16 *a*, 17 *a*. Total score 30. M.A. 10–6. IQ 81. (IQ computed on basis of 13–0.)

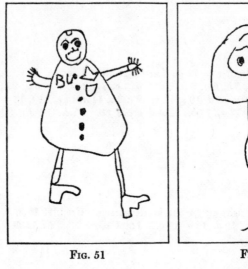

Fig. 51

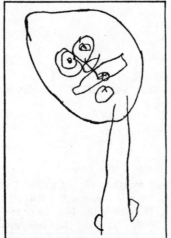

Fig. 53

Fig. 52

Fig. 54

Fig. 51. Boy, American, age 6–0, kindergarten. Credits, 1, 2, 3, 4 *a*, 5 *a*, 7 *a*, 7 *b*, 7 *c*, 7 *e*, 9 *a*, 10 *a*, 10 *e*, 12 *a*, 12 *e*, 13, 14 *a*, 16 *a*, 17 *a*. Total score 18. M.A. 7–6. IQ 125. (The forehead is shown by a semicircle at the top of the head.)

Fig. 52. Girl, American, age 5–3, kindergarten. Credits, 1, 2, 4 *a*, 4 *b*, 7 *a*, 7 *c*, 16 *b*, 17 *a*. Total score 8. M.A. 5–0. IQ 95. (The forehead is shown by a line above the eyes.)

Fig. 53. Boy, Italian, age 4–9, kindergarten. Credits, 1, 2, 7 *a*, 7 *b*, 7 *c*, 16 *b*, 17 *a*. Total score 7. M.A. 4–9. IQ 100. (The chin is shown by a circle below the mouth. The tongue also is shown.

Fig. 54. Girl, Jewish, age 5–8, pre-school. Credits, 1, 2, 3, 4 *a*, 5 *a*, 6 *a*, 7 *a*, 7 *b*, 7 *c*, 8 *a*, 10 *a*, 12 *b*, 12 *c*, 12 *e*, 15 *a*, 17 *a*. Total score 16. M.A. 7–0. IQ 124. (The forehead is shown by a line above the eyes.)

FIG. 55

FIG. 56

FIG. 57

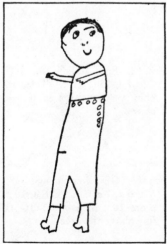

FIG. 58

Fig. 55. Girl, Egyptian, age 12–0, low fifth grade. Credits, 1, 2, 3, 4 *a*, 4 *c*, 5 *a*, 5 *b*, 6 *a*, 6 *b*, 7 *a*, 7 *b*, 7 *c*, 7 *e*, 8 *a*, 8 *b*, 9 *a*, 9 *b*, 9 *c*, 9 *d*, 9 *e*, 10 *a*, 10 *b*, 10 *c*, 11 *a*, 11 *b*, 12 *b*, 12 *c*, 12 *d*, 12 *e*, 13, 14 *a*, 14 *c*, 14 *d*, 14 *e*, 14 *f*, 15 *a*, 15 *b*, 16 *a*, 16 *b*, 16 *c*, 17 *a*. Total score 41. M.A. 13–0 or above. IQ 108 or above. Markedly "feminine" drawing. Note the large eyes, with much detail, nostrils, "cupid's bow" mouth, neatly parted hair, and laced shoes.

Fig. 56. Girl, Negro, age 10–9, high second grade. Credits, 1, 2, 3, 4 *a*, 5 *a*, 6 *a*, 7 *a*, 7 *b*, 7 *c*, 8 *a*, 9 *a*, 9 *b*, 10 *a*, 10 *e*, 11 *b*, 12 *b*, 12 *c*, 12 *e*, 14 *a*, 16 *a*, 16 *b*. Score 21. M.A. 8–3. IQ 77. Markedly "feminine." It will be noted that the eyes are larger than the feet. The drawing is remarkably "static" in type.

Fig. 57. Girl, Italian, age 8–0, low second grade. Credits, 1, 2, 3, 4 *a*, 5 *a*, 6 *a*, 7 *a*, 7 *b*, 7 *c*, 7 *e*, 8 *a*, 8 *b*, 9 *a*, 10 *a*, 10 *b*, 10 *e*, 11 *b*, 12 *c*, 12 *e*, 14 *a*, 16 *a*, 16 *b*, 16 *c*. Total score 23. M.A. 8–9. IQ 109. Markedly "feminine." Note the eye detail. The mouth as well as the nose is here shown only by two dots.

Fig. 58. Girl, Negro, age 8–2, high third grade. Credits, 1, 2, 3, 4 *a*, 4 *b*, 4 *c*, 5 *a*, 7 *a*, 7 *b*, 7 *c*, 7 *e*, 8 *a*, 8 *b*, 9 *a*, 10 *a*, 11 *b*, 12 *a*, 12 *d*, 12 *e*, 13, 14 *a*, 14 *d*, 16 *a*, 16 *b*, 16 *c*. Total score 25. M.A. 9–3. IQ 113. Markedly "feminine." Note the tiny arms and short legs, the nostrils, and the eye detail.

FIG. 59

FIG. 60

FIG. 61

FIG. 62

Fig. 59. Boy, Negro, age 12–10, low fourth grade. Credits, 1, 2, 3, 4 *a*, 4 *b*, 4 *c*, 5 *a*, 5 *b*, 6 *a*, 6 *b*, 7 *a*, 7 *b*, 7 *c*, 8 *a*, 9 *a*, 9 *d*, 10 *a*, 10 *b*, 10 *c*, 10 *e*, 11 *b*, 12 *a*, 12 *c*, 12 *d*, 12 *e*, 13, 14 *a*, 15 *a*, 15 *b*, 16 *a*, 17 *a*. Total score 31. M.A. 10–9. IQ 84. Markedly "masculine." Note the small head, the eyes shown only by a dot, the transparent clothing and large feet.

Fig. 60. Boy, Negro, age 9–6, high third grade. Credits, 1, 2, 3, 4 *a*, 4 *c*, 5 *a*, 5 *b*, 6 *a*, 6 *b*, 7 *a*, 7 *b*, 7 *c*, 9 *a*, 9 *b*, 9 *d*, 10 *a*, 10 *c*, 10 *e*, 11 *b*, 12 *a*, 12 *b*, 12 *d*, 12 *e*, 13, 14 *a*, 15 *a*, 16 *a*. Total score 27. M.A. 9–9. IQ 103. Markedly "masculine."

Fig. 61. Boy, American, age 12–9, high sixth grade. Credits, 1, 2, 3, 4 *a*, 4 *b*, 4 *c*, 5 *a*, 5 *b*, 6 *a*, 6 *b*, 7 *b*, 7 *c*, 8 *a*, 8 *b*, 9 *a*, 9 *d*, 10 *a*, 11 *a*, 11 *b*, 12 *a*, 12 *b*, 12 *e*, 13, 14 *a*, 14 *d*, 15 *a*, 16 *a*. Total score 27. M.A. 9–9. IQ 76. The brow is shown by the supra-orbital ridge, but there is no indication of the eye itself; the sleeves are not indicated. The drawing is markedly masculine in type.

Fig. 62. Boy, American, age 9–9, high fourth grade. Credits, 1, 2, 3, 4 *a*, 4 *b*, 4 *c*, 5 *a*, 5 *b*, 6 *a*, 7 *a*, 7 *b*, 7 *c*, 7 *d*, 8 *a*, 9 *a*, 9 *d*, 10 *a*, 10 *c*, 11 *b*, 12 *b*, 12 *e*, 13, 14 *a*, 14 *f*, 15 *a*, 15 *b*, 16 *a*, 16 *b*, 16 *c*, 17 *a*, 17 *b*. Total score 31. M.A. 10–9. IQ 110. One of the drawings selected as showing psychopathic features in the experiment described in Chapter III. Note the "individual" characteristics, the large amount of apparently meaningless detail-"verbalism" and compare the maturity of the face with the primitive drawing of the neck and trunk. This child was described by the teachers as *timid, unstable, concentrates poorly, peculiar, placid,* and *stubborn.*

Fig. 63

Fig. 64

Fig. 65

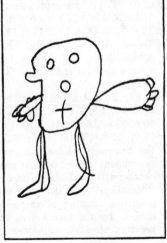

Fig. 66

Fɪɢ. 63. Boy, American, age 8–2, low first grade. Credits, 2, 7 *a*, 7 *b*, 7 *c*, 8 *a*, 10 *a*, 16 *a*. Total score 7. M.A. 4–9. IQ 58. The child's mother is insane, and there are other cases of insanity reported in the family. Child's conduct was such that he was twice excluded from school, but at the time the drawing was made he had been reinstated under the care of a very sympathetic teacher and was doing somewhat better. He was not, however, conforming to the ordinary schoolroom rules, was highly erratic and excitable, could not be kept quiet, and had made no progress in school work beyond learning to recognize half a dozen words at sight. His Stanford-Binet IQ was 69; drawing IQ 58. The drawing shows a remarkable lack of coherence; far greater than that ordinarily found even in drawings by the feeble-minded. The fingers are attached to the eyes; the legs suspended from the mouth.

Fɪɢ. 64. Girl, English, age 6–8, low first grade. Credits, 1, 2, 3, 4 *a*, 4 *b*, 7 *a*, 7 *b*, 7 *c*, 9 *a*, 10 *a*, 15 *a*. Total score 11. M.A. 5–9. IQ 86. The child has a normal heredity and is reported to have developed normally up to the age of two and a half years, at which time she had a very severe attack of what was probably encephalitis. Upon recovery, she had lost the power of speech (she had talked very well before her illness), seemed unable to orient herself at all, but would walk in whatever direction she happened to be facing until she was stopped and brought back. She gradually relearned to talk but continued to be very flighty and unstable, and could not be trusted out of doors by herself. She was retained in school only a short time. The psychopathic indications in the drawing are hard to define. They consist chiefly in an instability of line; and in much apparently meaningless detail similar to that shown in Figure 63, although the drawing is of a much more primitive type. The two black dots indicate the cheeks; the circles above them are the eyes.

Fɪɢ. 65. Boy, American, age 11–1, high fifth grade. Credits, 1, 2, 3, 4 *a*, 4 *b*, 5 *a*, 5 *b*, 6 *a*, 6 *b*, 7 *a*, 7 *b*, 7 *c*, 7 *d*, 8 *a*, 8 *b*, 9 *a*, 9 *d*, 10 *a*, 10 *c*, 11 *a*, 11 *b*, 12 *a*, 12 *d*, 12 *e*, 13, 14 *a*, 16 *b*, 16 *c*, 17 *a*, 17 *b*. Total score 30. M.A. 10–6. IQ 95. Selected in the experiment described in Chapter III. Note the unexplained vertical bars on the arms and the inverted figures at the side, as well as the pronounced "verbalism" shown in the entire drawing. This child was described by the teacher as "too" *courageous, apathetic, suspicious, easily depressed, active, enthusiastic "at times," dreamy, unstable, flighty, oversensitive, self-conscious, concentrates poorly, fond of companionship, peculiar, shows good common sense, modest, boastful, restless, stubborn, muscles twitch, healthy.*

Fɪɢ. 66. Boy, Negro, age 6–5, low first grade. Credits, 1, 2, 3, 7 *a*, 7 *b*, 7 *c*, 9 *a*, 10 *a*, 12 *e*, 14 *a*. Total score 10. M.A. 5–6. IQ 86. The extra lines on the legs indicate the trousers. The mouth is shown by a cross.

FIG. 67

FIG. 68

FIG. 69

FIG. 70

FIG. 67. Girl, Negro, age 8–7, low first grade. Credits, 1, 2, 3, 7 *a*, 9 *a*, 10 *a*, 10 *c*, 12 *e*, 14 *a*, 16 *b*. Total score 10. M.A. 5–6. IQ 64. The lines enclosing the arms indicate the sleeves.

FIG. 68. Girl, Negro, age 6–5, low first grade. Credits, 1, 2, 3, 4 *a*, 7 *a*, 8 *a*, 10 *a*. Total score 7. M.A. 4–9. IQ 74. The scribbled line above the head is the hair. The two dots below the eyes are the cheeks. (Where the head and trunk are included in one figure, as in this instance, points 12 *a*, 12 *b*, and 12 *c* automatically become zero, since it is impossible to tell where the division between head and trunk should be made.)

FIG. 69. Boy, Italian, age 6–8, low first grade. Credits, 1, 2, 3, 4 *a*, 7 *a*, 7 *b*, 7 *c*, 8 *a*, 9 *a*, 10 *a*, 12 *c*, 16 *a*. Total score 12. M.A. 6–0. IQ 90. The hair is shown by the circle of little spirals surrounding the head. Note that an inverted heel such as that shown on the foot on the left is not credited for point 13.

FIG. 70. Boy, American, age 7–4, high first grade. Credits, 1, 2, 3, 4 *a*, 4 *b*, 5 *a*, 7 *a*, 7 *b*, 7 *c*, 8 *a*, 9 *a*, 10 *a*, 10 *b*, 12 *d*, 12 *e*, 14 *a*, 16 *b*. Total score 17. M.A. 7–3. IQ 99. Lack of foresight in placing the drawing on the paper accounts for the peculiarities in this picture. Notice the short arm on the left, and the infinitesimal hat, which the child was unwilling to omit in spite of the lack of space.

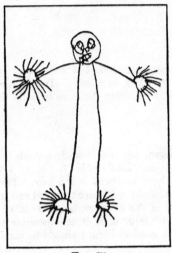

FIG. 71

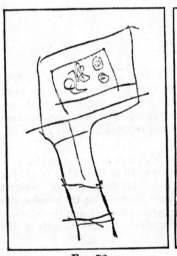

FIG. 72

FIG. 73

FIG. 71. Girl, American, age 5–4, kindergarten. Credits, 1, 2, 3, 7 *a*, 7 *b*, 7 *c*, 10 *a*, 10 *e*. Total score 8. M.A. 5–0. IQ 94. This represents approximately the upper limit of failure for point 17 *a*. The scribbled outline of the eye does not indicate the pupil.

FIG. 72. Girl, Jewish, age 4–11, pre-school. Credits, 1, 2, 4 *a*, 4 *b*, 7 *a*, 7 *b*, 7 *c*, 16 *b*. Total score 8. M.A. 5–0. IQ 102. Compare the drawing of the pupil of the eye with the preceding figure. Note that here it is entirely distinct from the outline of the eye in one case and well separated from the outline in the other. The inner square represents the face.

FIG. 73. Girl, Italian, age 6–9, kindergarten. Credits, 1, 2, 3, 4 *a*, 5 *a*, 6 *a*, 7 *a*, 7 *b*, 7 *c*, 7 *d*, 10 *a*, 12 *c*, 12 *e*. Total score 13. M.A. 6–3. IQ 93. The circle around the features signifies the face. The small circle within the trunk is the stomach.

FIG. 74   FIG. 75

FIG. 76   FIG. 77

Fig. 74. Girl, Italian, age 6–11, low first grade. Credits, 1, 2, 3, 4 *a*, 5 *a*, 7 *a*, 7 *b*, 9 *a*, 12 *e*. Total score 9. M.A. 5–3. IQ 76. The enormous protuberance extending out from the head was said by the child to be the nose. Ordinarily it would be safe to interpret such a feature as the other arm. There was nothing in the child's manner or behavior to indicate that a caricature had been intended; she seemed very complacent about her work.

Fig. 75. Girl, Japanese, age 5–3, kindergarten. Credits, 1, 7 *a*, 7 *b*, 7 *c*. Total score 4. M.A. 4–0. IQ 76.

Fig. 76. Boy, Italian, age 4–4, pre-school. Credits, 1, 2, 7 *a*, 16 *a*. Total score 4. M.A. 4–0. IQ 92.

Fig. 77. Girl, racial stock unknown, age 5–10, low first grade. Credits, 1, 2, 7 *a*, 7 *b*, 7 *c*, 9 *a*. Total score 6. M.A. 4–6. IQ 77. Through a mistake, crayon was used for this drawing in place of pencil, but it is unlikely that its use has affected the results, since the drawing is of so primitive a type.

FIG. 78   FIG. 79

FIG. 80   FIG. 81

Fig. 78. Boy, American, age 9–3, low fourth grade. Credits, 1, 2, 3, 4 *a*, 5 *a*, 7 *a*, 7 *b*, 7 *c*, 9 *a*, 10 *a*, 10 *b*, 12 *b*, 12 *c*, 12 *d*, 14 *a*, 15 *a*. Total score 16. M.A. 7–0. IQ 76. A delinquent; steals, lies, sex misconduct.

Fig. 79. Girl, Jewish, age 9–3, low third grade. Credits, 1, 2, 3, 4 *a*, 5 *a*, 6 *a*, 6 *b*, 7 *a*, 7 *b*, 7 *e*, 9 *a*, 9 *b*, 9 *d*, 11 *a*, 11 *b*, 12 *e*, 13. 14 *a*, 16 *a*. Total score 19. M.A. 7–9. IQ 84.

Fig. 80. Boy, Indian, age 7–3, first grade. Credits, 1, 2, 3, 4 *a*, 4 *b*, 5 *a*, 7 *a*, 9 *a*, 10 *a*, 12 *c*, 13. Total score 11. M.A. 5–9. IQ 79.

Fig. 81. Girl, American, age 9–5, low fourth grade. Credits, 1, 2, 3, 4 *a*, 5 *a*, 6 *a*, 7 *a*, 7 *b*, 7 *c*, 7 *e*, 8 *a*, 9 *a*, 10 *a*, 10 *b*, 12 *a*, 12 *c*, 12 *d*. 12 *e*, 14 *a*, 16 *a*, 17 *a*. Total score 21. M.A. 8–3. IQ 88.

SCORING KEY FOR SPECIMEN DRAWINGS

Series II

TEST EXERCISE

This series of drawings has been included in order to provide the student with a means for gauging his mastery of the directions for scoring. After the prospective scorer has thoroughly familiarized himself with the rules given in Chapter VII, and has checked through the scoring of the specimen drawings in Series I, the drawings in Series II should be scored independently. A point-for-point comparison should then be made with the standard scores for these drawings which is given on pages 160–161. If the total error does not exceed one or two points, it will ordinarily be safe for him to begin regular scoring, provided that he proceed rather carefully in the beginning and refer to the guide for help in all doubtful points.

FIG. 82   FIG. 83

FIG. 84   FIG. 85

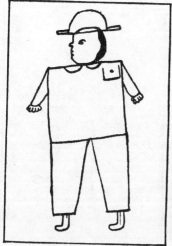

FIG. 86

FIG. 87

FIG. 88

FIG. 89

Fig. 90

Fig. 91

Fig. 92

Fig. 93

FIG. 94

FIG. 95

FIG. 96

FIG. 97

FIG. 82. Boy, Italian, age 6–4, high first grade. Credits, 1, 2, 4 *a*, 7 *a*, 7 *b*, 7 *c*, 9 *a*, 14 *a*, 16 *b*, 16 *c*, 17 *a*.   Total score 11.   M.A. 5–9.   IQ 91.

FIG. 83. Girl, Mexican, age 10–3, low second grade. Credits, 1, 2, 3, 4 *a*, 4 *b*, 5 *a*, 5 *b*, 7 *a*, 7 *b*, 7 *c*, 7 *e*, 9 *a*, 9 *b*, 9 *c*, 9 *d*, 10 *a*, 10 *e*, 11 *b*, 12 *e*, 14 *a*, 16 *a*, 16 *b*, 16 *c*, 17 *a*.   Total score 24. M.A. 9–0.   IQ 88.

FIG. 84. Girl, American, age 5–1, kindergarten. Credits, 1, 2, 3, 4 *a*, 5 *a*, 7 *a*, 7 *b*, 7 *c*, 7 *e*, 8 *a*, 10 *a*, 16 *a*, 17 *a*.   Total score 13. M.A. 6–3.   IQ 123.

FIG. 85. Girl, American, age 8–4, high second grade. Credits, 1, 2, 3, 4 *a*, 4 *b*, 4 *c*, 5 *a*, 5 *b*, 6 *a*, 6 *b*, 7 *a*, 7 *b*, 7 *c*, 7 *e*, 8 *a*, 9 *a*, 9 *b*, 9 *d*, 11 *b*, 12 *a*, 12 *b*, 12 *c*, 12 *d*, 12 *e*, 13, 14 *a*, 14 *d*, 15 *a*, 15 *b*, 16 *a*, 16 *b*, 17 *a*.   Total score 32.   M.A. 11–0.   IQ 132.

FIG. 86. Girl, Negro, age 13–1, high fourth grade. Credits, 1, 2, 3, 4 *a*, 5 *a*, 5 *b*, 7 *a*, 7 *b*, 7 *c*, 8 *a*, 8 *b*, 9 *a*, 9 *b*, 10 *a*, 10 *b*, 10 *c*, 10 *e*, 11 *b*, 12 *a*, 12 *c*, 12 *d*, 12 *e*, 14 *a*, 14 *c*, 14 *e*, 16 *a*, 17 *a*, 17 *b*.   Total score 28.   M.A. 10–0.   IQ 77.   Note that coat lapels may not be counted as collar.

FIG. 87. Boy, Italian, age 8–4, low first grade. Credits, 1, 2, 3, 7 *a*, 7 *b*, 7 *c*, 7 *e*, 8 *a*, 10 *a*, 10 *b*.   Total score 10.   M.A. 5–6. IQ 66.   An example of a very feminine drawing made by a boy.

FIG. 88. Boy, American, age 5–8, kindergarten. Credits, 1, 2, 3, 4 *a*, 5 *a*, 7 *a*, 7 *b*, 7 *c*, 10 *a*, 12 *a*, 12 *c*.   Total score 11.   M.A. 5–9.   IQ 102.

FIG. 89. Boy, Italian, age 5–10, kindergarten. Credits, 1, 2, 3, 7 *a*, 8 *a*, 9 *a*, 10 *a*.   Total score 7.   M.A. 4–9.   IQ 81.

Fig. 90. Girl, Negro, age 6–2, low first grade. Credits, 1, 2, 3, 7 *a*. Total score 4. M.A. 4–0. IQ 65.

Fig. 91. Girl, Mexican, age 5–9, kindergarten. Credits, 1, 2, 3, 7 *a*, 7 *b*, 7 *c*, 10 *a*, 15 *a*, 16 *a*, 17 *a*. Total score 10. M.A. 5–6. IQ 96.

Fig. 92. Boy, Indian, age 10–3, second grade. (Larger drawing scored.) Credits, 1, 2, 3, 4 *a*, 4 *b*, 4 *c*, 5 *a*, 6 *a*, 7 *a*, 7 *b*, 7 *c*, 7 *e*, 9 *a*, 10 *a*, 10 *b*, 10 *c*, 12 *a*, 12 *b*, 12 *c*, 12 *e*, 13, 14 *a*, 15 *a*, 16 *a*. Total score 24. M.A. 9–0. IQ 88.

Fig. 93. Girl, American, age 5–11, kindergarten. Credits, 1, 2, 3, 4 *a*, 4 *b*, 5 *a*, 7 *a*, 7 *b*, 7 *c*, 9 *a*, 10 *e*, 12 *c*, 14 *a*, 15 *a*. Total score 14. M.A. 6–6. IQ 110.

Fig. 94. Boy, Irish, age 5–11, kindergarten. Credits, 1, 2, 3, 4 *a*, 4 *b*, 5 *a*, 7 *a*, 7 *b*, 7 *c*, 8 *a*, 9 *a*, 10 *a*. Total score 12. M.A. 6–0. IQ 102. A curious confusion with regard to the number of fingers is present here. Each arm terminates in two groups of five fingers each.

Fig. 95. Boy, American, age 6–1, kindergarten. Credits, 1, 2, 7 *a*, 7 *b*, 7 *c*, 7 *e*, 12 *d*, 17 *a*. Total score 8. M.A. 5–0. IQ 82.

Fig. 96. Boy, Italian, age 5–6, kindergarten. Credits, 1, 2, 7 *a*, 7 *c*. Total score 4. M.A. 4–0. IQ 73.

Fig. 97. Boy, American, age 6–3, high first grade. Credits, 1, 2, 3, 4 *a*, 4 *b*, 5 *a*, 6 *a*, 7 *a*, 7 *b*, 7 *c*, 9 *a*, 10 *a*, 10 *b*, 10 *c*, 10 *e*, 12 *b*, 12 *c*, 12 *e*. Total score 18. M.A. 7–6. IQ 120.

BIBLIOGRAPHY

Children's Drawings

1. ALBIEN, GUSTAV. "Der Anteil der nachkonstruierenden Tätigkeit des Auges und der Apperception an dem Behalten und der Wiedergabe einfacher Formen." *Zeitschrift für experimentelle Pädagogik*, Vol. 5 (1907), pages 133–156, and Vol. 6 (1908), pages 1–48.

2. AMENT, WILHELM. "Fortschritte der Kinderseelenkunde," in *Sammlung von psychologischen Pädagogik* by Meumann, Vol. 1. 1905. 76 pages. (See especially pages 10–11 and 35–36.)

3. AYER, F. C. *The Psychology of Drawing*. Warwick & York, Inc., Baltimore. 1916.

4. —— "The Present Status of Instruction in Drawing with Respect to Scientific Investigation." *Yearbook of the National Society for the Study of Education*, Vol. 18 (1919), pages 96–110.

5. BALLARD, P. B. "What London Children Like to Draw." *Journal of Experimental Pedagogy*, Vol. 1 (1912), pages 185–197.

6. —— "What Children Like to Draw." *Journal of Experimental Pedagogy*, Vol. 2 (1913), pages 127–129.

7. BARNES, EARL. "A Study of Children's Drawings." *Pedagogical Seminary*, Vol. 2 (1893), pages 451–463.

8. —— "Notes on Children's Drawings." *Pedagogical Seminary*, Vol. 1 (1891), pages 445–447.

9. —— *Studies in Education*, Vol. 1. 1899. (See pages 23, 63, 105, 155, 180, 227, 265, 341, 367.)

10. BECHTEREW, W. "Recherches Objectives sur l'Évolution du Dessin chez l'Enfant." *Journal de Psychologie Normale et Pathologique*, Vol. 8 (1911), pages 385–405.

11. BELOT, G. "Dessins d'Enfants." *Bulletin Société Étude Psychologique de l'Enfant*, Vol. 1 (1901), pages 50–59.

12. —— "Les Études Relatives à la Psychologie de l'Enfant." *Bulletin Société Étude Psychologique de l'Enfant*, Vol. 7 (1907), pages 121–144.

13. BENCINI, PAOLA. "I Disegni dei Fanciulli." *Rivista Pedagogia*, Vol. 1 (1908), pages 665–690.

14. BESNARD, A. "Dessins d'Enfants." *Revue Universelle*, Vol. 1 (1901), pages 817–823.

15. —— "Dessins d'Enfants." *Bulletin Société Étude Psychologique de l'Enfant*, Vol. 2 (1902), pages 162–169.

16. BOUBIER, A. M. "Les Jeux de l'Enfant pendant la Classe." *Archives de Psychologie*, Vol. 1 (1902), pages 44–68.

17. BROWN, D. D. "Notes on Children's Drawings." *University of California Publications* (1897).

18. BURK, FREDERICK. "The Genetic *vs.* the Logical Order in Drawing." *Pedagogical Seminary*, Vol. 9 (1902), pages 296–323.

19. BURT, CYRIL. *Mental and Scholastic Tests.* Report of the London County Council. 1921.

20. BUSEMAN, K. U. A. "Über das Zeichnen nach Vorlage." *Zeitschrift für Kinderforschung,* Vol. 20 (1915), pages 518–530.

21. CHAMBERLAIN, A. F. *The Child: A Study in the Evolution of Man.* Charles Scribner's Sons, New York. 1900. (See Chapter VI.)

22. CHILDS, H. G. "Measurement of the Drawing Ability of 2177 Children in Indiana City School Systems by a Supplemented Thorndike Scale." *Journal of Educational Psychology,* Vol. 6 (1915), pages 391–408.

23. CLAPARÈDE, E. "Plan d'Expériences Collectives sur le Dessin des Enfants." *Archives de Psychologie,* Vol. 6 (1907), pages 276–278.

24. CLARK, A. B. "The Child's Attitude toward Perspective Problems," in *Studies in Education* by Barnes, Vol. 1 (1902), pages 283–294.

25. CLARK, J. S. "Some Observations on Children's Drawings." *Educational Review,* Vol. 13 (1897), pages 76–82.

26. CLAUS, A. "Psychologische Betrachtungen zür Methodik des Zeichenunterrichts." *Zeitschrift für pädagogische Psychologie,* Vol. 3 (1901), pages 456–473.

27. COHEN, JOSEPH. "The Use of Objective Criteria in the Measurement of Drawing Ability." *Pedagogical Seminary,* Vol. 27 (1920), pages 137–151.

28. COOKE, EBENEZER. "Art Teaching and Child Nature." *London Journal of Education* (1885).

29. DARWIN, CHARLES. "A Biographical Sketch of an Infant." *Mind,* Vol. 2 (1877), pages 285–294.

30. DE BRUIN, W. K. "De Perspectief in het Naiefteekenen." *School en Leven,* Vol. 2 (1901), pages 828–832.

31. DECROLY, O. "La Psychologie du Dessin." *Journal de Neurologie,* Vol. 17 (1912), pages 421–424 and 441–453.

32. DIX, K. W. *Körperliche und geistige Entwicklung eines Kindes.* Leipzig. 1912. 174 pages. (See pages 67–96.)

33. DUCK, JOHANNES. "Über das Zeichnerische und künstlerische Interesse der Schüler." *Zeitschrift für pädagogische Psychologie,* Vol. 13 (1912), pages 172–177.

34. ELDERTON, ETHEL. "On the Association of Drawing with Other Aptitudes in School Children." *Biometrika,* Vol. 7 (1909), pages 222–226.

35. GAUPP, R. *Psychologie des Kindes.* Leipzig. 1912. 163 pages. (See especially pages 131–145.)

36. GÖTZE, K. *Das Kind als Künstler.* Hamburg. 1898.

37. GRABERG, F. "Die visuell-motorischen Zeichnenvorgänge." *Zeitschrift für experimentelle Pädagogik,* Vol. 7 (1908), pages 68–92.

38. —— "Kraftsteigern des Zeichnen." *Zeitschrift für experimentelle Pädagogik,* Vol. 8 (1909), pages 104–113.

39. GRABERG, F. "Eine Stufenfolge von Masszeichen." *Zeitschrift für experimentelle Pädagogik*, Vol. 4 (1907), pages 175–188.

40. —— "Zeichnen, Sprechen, Rechnen." *Zeitschrift für experimentelle Pädagogik*, Vol. 9 (1909), pages 149–168.

41. GROSSER, H., and STERN, W. *Das freie Zeichnen und Formen des Kindes.* Leipzig. 1913.

42. GUYER, WALTER. "Kind und Künstler." *Schweizerische pädagogische Zeitschrift*, Vol. 32 (1922), pages 161–168.

43. HASSERODT, O. "Bilderunterricht." *Zeitschrift für pädagogische Psychologie*, Vol. 14 (1913), pages 210–222 and 276–290.

44. HERRICK, MARY A. "Children's Drawings." *Pedagogical Seminary*, Vol. 3 (1893), pages 338–339.

45. HICKS, MARY DANA. "Art in Early Education." *Kindergarten Magazine*, Vol. 6 (1894), pages 590–605.

46. HOGAN, LOUISE. *A Study of a Child.* Harper & Brothers, New York. 1898.

47. HOLLINGWORTH, L. S. *Psychology of Subnormal Children.* The Macmillan Company, New York. 1920. (See pages 183–184.)

48. —— *Special Talents and Defects; Their Significance for Education.* The Macmillan Company, New York. 1923. (See especially Chapter VII.)

49. HORNIG, REINHOLD. "Zeichen und Schreibphänomene bei Elementarschülern." *Zeitschrift für angewandte Psychologie*, Vol. 3 (1910), pages 541–545.

50. HUG-HELLMUTH, H. *Aus dem Seelenleben des Kindes.* Leipzig. 1913. (See especially pages 151–163.)

51. IVANOFF, E. "Recherches Expérimentales sur le Dessin des Écoliers de la Suisse Romande: Correlation entre l'Aptitude au Dessin et les Autres Aptitudes." *Archives de Psychologie*, Vol. 8 (1909), pages 97–156.

52. JACOBS, ÉMILE. "Contributions a l'Étude Psychologique de l'Enfant: Le Langage Graphique de Rouma." *Revue Psychologique*, Vol. 6 (1913), page 363.

53. JESSEN, PETER. "Die Erziehung zur bildenen Kunst." *Zeitschrift für pädagogische Psychologie*, Vol. 4 (1902), pages 1–10.

54. KARRENBERG, C. *Der Mensch als Zeichenobjekt.* Leipzig. 1910.

55. KATZ, DAVID. "Ein Beitrag zur Kenntnis der Kinderzeichnungen." *Zeitschrift für Psychologie und Physiologie der Sinnesorgane*, Vol. 41 (1906), pages 241–256.

56. KATZAROFF, M. D. "Qu'est ce que les Enfants Dessinent?" *Archives de Psychologie*, Vol. 9 (1910), page 125.

57. KERSCHENSTEINER, D. G. *Die Entwickelung der zeichnerischen Begabung.* Gerber. Münich. 1905.

58. KIK, C. "Die übernormal Zeichenbegabung bei Kindern." *Zeitschrift für angewandte Psychologie*, Vol. 2 (1909), pages 92–149.

59. KLINE, L. W., and CAREY, GERTRUDE L. "A Measuring Scale for Freehand Drawing." *Johns Hopkins Studies in Education*, No. 5. 1922. 60 pages.

60. KRETZCHMAR, JOHANNES. "Die Sammlung von Kinderzeichnungen des Instituts für Kultur- und Universalgeschichte bei der Universität Leipzig." *Zeitschrift für angewandte Psychologie*, Vol. 3 (1910), pages 459–463.

61. —— "Die freie Kinderzeichnung in der wissenschaftlichen Forschung." *Zeitschrift für pädagogische Psychologie*, Vol. 13 (1912), pages 380–396.

62. LEVINSTEIN, S. *Kinderzeichnungen bis zum 14 Lebensjahre. Mit Parallelen aus der Urgeschichte, Kulturgeschichte, und Völkerkunde.* Voigtländer. Leipzig. 1905. 169 pages.

63. LINDNER, RUDOLF. "Die Einführung in die Schriftsprache." *Zeitschrift für pädagogische Psychologie*, Vol. 11 (1910), pages 177–205.

64. —— "Wiederholung eines Zeichnenversuches Kerschensteiners in der Taubstummenschule." *Zeitschrift für pädagogische Psychologie*, Vol. 13 (1912), pages 419–421.

65. —— "Moralpsychologische Auswertung freier Kinderzeichnungen von taubstummen Schülern." *Zeitschrift für pädagogische Psychologie*, Vol. 15 (1914), pages 160–177.

66. LOBSIEN, MARX. "Kinderzeichnung und Kunstkanon." *Zeitschrift für pädagogische Psychologie*, Vol. 7 (1905), pages 393–404.

67. LOCKE, JOSEPHINE. "With What Should Drawing Begin?" *Proceedings of the National Education Association* (1893), page 491.

68. LOMBROSO, PAOLA. *Das Leben der Kinder.* (Autorisierte Übersetzung von Helene Goldbaum.) Leipzig. 1909. 111 pages. (See especially Chapter V.)

69. LORENT, H. "Sur une Methode Synthetique de Dessin d'apres Nature." *Revue Psychologique*, Vol. 4 (1911), pages 345–357.

70. LUKENS, H. "A Study of Children's Drawing in the Early Years." *Pedagogical Seminary*, Vol. 4 (1896), pages 79–110.

71. LUQUET, G. H. "Le Premier Age du Dessin Enfantin." *Archives de Psychologie*, Vol. 12 (1912), pages 14–20.

72. —— *Les Dessins d'un Enfant.* Paris. 1913.

73. —— "Les Bonhommes Tetards dans le Dessin Enfantin." *Journal de Psychologie Normale et Pathologie*, Vol. 17 (1920), pages 684–710.

74. MAITLAND, LOUISE. "What Children Draw to Please Themselves." *Inland Educator*, Vol. 1 (1895), page 87.

75. MANSON, J. B. "The Drawings of Pamela Bianca." *International Studio*, Vol. 68 (1919), pages 119–125.

76. MANUEL, H. *A Study of Talent in Drawing.* School and Home Education Monograph No. 3. Public School Publishing Company, Bloomington, Illinois. 1919.

77. MATZ, W. "Zeichen und Modellierversuch an Volksschülern, Hilfsschülern, Taubstummen, und Blinden." *Zeitschrift für angewandte Psychologie*, Vol. 10 (1915), pages 62–135.

78. MEUMANN, ERNST. *Vorlesungen zur Einführung in die experimentelle Pädagogik*, Vol. 2. Leipzig. 1907. (See pages 360–397.)

79. —— "Ein Programm zur psychologische Untersuchung des Zeichnens." *Zeitschrift für pädagogische Psychologie*, Vol. 13 (1912), pages 353–380.

80. MUTH, G. F. "Über Ornamentationsversuche mit Kindern im Alter von sechs bis zehn Jahren." *Zeitschrift für angewandte Psychologie*, Vol. 7 (1913), pages 223–271.

81. —— "Über Ornamentationsversuche mit Kindern im Alter von sechs bis neun Jahren." *Zeitschrift für angewandte Psychologie*, Vol. 6 (1912), pages 21–50.

82. OGDEN, R. M. "The Pictorial Representation of Distance." *Psychological Bulletin*, Vol. 5 (1908), pages 109–113.

83. O'SHEA, M. V. "Some Aspects of Drawing." *Educational Review*, Vol. 14 (1897), pages 263–284.

84. —— *Mental Development and Education*. The Macmillan Company, New York. 1921. 403 pages. (See especially Chapter VI.)

85. —— "Children's Expression through Drawing." *Proceedings of the National Education Association* (1894), page 1015.

86. PAPPENHEIM, KARL. "Bemerkungen über Kinderzeichnungen." *Zeitschrift für pädagogische Psychologie*, Vol. 1 (1899), pages 57–73.

87. —— "Das Tierzeichnen der Kinder." *Kindergarten*, Vol. 41 (1900), pages 180–182 and 247–252.

88. —— "Die Kinderzeichnung im Anschauungsunterricht." *Zeitschrift für pädagogische Psychologie*, Vol. 2 (1900), pages 161–190.

89. PARTRIDGE, LENA. "Children's Drawings of Men and Women," in *Studies in Education* by Barnes, Vol. 2 (1902), pages 163–179.

90. PAULSSON, GREGOR. "The Creative Element in Art." *Scandinavian Scientific Review*, Vol. 2 (1923), pages 11–173.

91. PEREZ, M. B. *L'Art et la Poesie chez l'Enfant*. Paris. 1888. (See Chapter VI.)

92. —— *L'Éducation intellectualle dés le Berceau*. Alcan, Paris. 1901. (See Chapter X.)

93. PETER, RUDOLF. "Beiträge zur Analyse der zeichnerischen Begabung." *Zeitschrift für pädagogische Psychologie*, Vol. 15 (1914), pages 96–104.

94. PINTNER, RUDOLF, and TOOPS, H. A. "A Drawing Completion Test." *Journal of Applied Psychology*, Vol. 2 (1918), pages 164–173.

95. PREYER, WILHELM. *The Mind of the Child* (tr. by W. H. Brown). D. Appleton & Co., New York. 1899.

96. RICCI, CORRADO. *L'Arte dei Bambini*. Bologna, 1887. (Tr. by Maitland in *Pedagogical Seminary*, Vol. 3 (1894), pages 302–307.)

97. ROUMA, GEORGES. *Le Langage Graphique de l'Enfant*. Misch et Thron, Paris. 1913.

98. RUTTMAN, W. J. *Die Ergebnisse der Bisherigen Untersuchungen zur Psychologie des Zeichnens*. Wunderlich, Leipzig. 1911.

99. SARGENT, WALTER. "Problems in the Experimental Pedagogy of Drawing." *Journal of Educational Psychology*, Vol. 3 (1912), pages 264–276.

100. SCHREUDER, A. J. "Über Kinderzeichnungen." *Zeitschrift für Kinderforschung*, Vol. 7 (1902), pages 216–229.

101. SCHUBERT, R. "Einige Aufgabe der Kinderforschung auf dem Gebiete der künstlerischen Erziehung." *Zeitschrift für pädagogische Psychologie*, Vol. 6 (1904), page 395.

102. SCHULZE, RUDOLF. *Experimental Psychology and Pedagogy* (tr. by Rudolf Pintner). George Allen & Unwin, London. 1912. (See pages 102–109.)

103. SCHUYTEN, M. C. "Note Pedagogique sur le Dessins des Enfants." *Archives de Psychologie*, Vol. 6 (1907), pages 389–391.

104. —— "Het Oorspronkelijk Teekenen als Bijdrage tot Kinderanalyse." *Paedologisch Jaarboek*, Vol. 2 (1901), pages 112–126.

105. —— "De oorspronkelijke 'Ventjes' der Antwerpsche Schoolkindern." *Paedologisch Jaarboek*, Vol. 5 (1904), pages 1–87.

106. SHINN, M. W. *Notes on the Development of a Child*. (In monograph by D. D. Brown.) University of California Studies. University of California, Berkeley, California. 1897.

107. SIKORSKY, J. A. *Die Seele des Kindes*. 1902. Leipzig. (See pages 59–61.)

108. STERN, CLARA and WILLIAM. "Die zeichnerische Entwickelung einer Knaben von 4 bis 7 Jahre." *Zeitschrift für angewandte Psychologie*, Vol. 3 (1910), pages 1–31.

109. STERN, WILLIAM. "Die Entwickelung der Raumwahrnehmung in der ersten Kindheit." *Zeitschrift für angewandte Psychologie*, Vol. 2 (1909), page 412.

110. —— *Psychologie der frühen Kindheit*. Leipzig. 1914. (See Chapter XX.)

111. —— "Spezielle Beschreibung der Ausstellung freier Kinderzeichnungen aus Breslau." *Bericht über den Kongress für Kinderforschung und Jugendfursorge in Berlin* (1907), pages 411–417.

112. STERN, KOHLER, and VERWORN. "Sammlungen freier Kinderzeichnungen." *Zeitschrift für angewandte Psychologie*, Vol. 1 (1908), pages 179–187 and 472–476.

113. STRYIENSKI, CASIMIR. "Dessins de Gens de Lettres." *Revue Universelle*, Vol. 1 (1901), pages 337–343.

114. SULLY, JAMES. *Children's Ways*. D. Appleton & Co., New York. 1907. (See Chapter XII.)

115. —— *Studies of Childhood*. D. Appleton & Co., New York. 1908.

116. TANNER, AMY E. *The Child: His Thinking, Feeling, and Doing*. Rand McNally & Co., Chicago. 1904. (See Chapter XIX.)

117. THORNDIKE, E. L. "The Measurement of Achievement in Drawing." *Teachers College Record*, Vol. 14, No. 5 (1913). Teachers College, Columbia University, New York.

118. THYZA and WIJT. "Kinderteekenen." *Vaktijdschrift voor Onderwijzers*, Vol. 8 (1904), pages 171–182.
119. ——— "Kinderteekenen." *Vaktijdschrift voor Onderwijzers*, Vol. 9 (1905), pages 7–29.
120. WAGNER, P. A. "Das freie Zeichnen von Volksschulkindern." *Zeitschrift für angewandte Psychologie*, Vol. 8 (1913), pages 1–70.
121. WEGLEIN, D. E. *The Correlation of Abilities of High School Pupils.* Johns Hopkins Studies in Education, No. 1. Johns Hopkins Press, Baltimore. 1917. 100 pages.
122. WISCHER, PAUL. "Zur Auswahl und Prüfung der zeichnerische Begabung." *Zeitschrift für pädagogische Psychologie*, Vol. 20 (1919), pages 219–231.

Drawings by the Insane

123. DE FURSAC, ROGUES. *Les Ecrits et les Dessins dans les Maladies Nerveuses et Mentales.* Masson, Paris. 1905.
124. HAMILTON, A. M. "Insane Art." *Scribner's Magazine*, Vol. 63 (1918), pages 484–492.
125. KURBITZ, W. "Die Zeichnungen geisteskranker Personen." *Zeitschrift für die gesammte Neurologie und Psychiatry*, Vol. 13 (1912), pages 153–182.
126. MATEER, FLORENCE. *The Unstable Child.* D. Appleton & Co., New York. 1924.
127. MOHR, H. "Zeichnungen von Geisteskranken." *Zeitschrift für angewandte Psychologie*, Vol. 2 (1909), pages 291–300.
128. REJA, MARCEL. "L'Arte Malade: Dessins de Fous." *Revue Universelle*, Vol. 1 (1901), pages 913–915 and 940–944.
129. ROUMA, GEORGES. "Un Cas de Mythomanie." *Archives de Psychologie*, Vol. 7 (1908), pages 258–282.

Art of Primitive Peoples

130. BALDWIN, J. M. *Mental Development in the Child and in the Race.* The Macmillan Company, New York. 1894.
131. BOUMAN, K. HERMAN. "Das biogenetische Grundgesetz und die Psychologie der primitiven bildenden Kunst." *Zeitschrift für angewandte Psychologie*, Vol. 14 (1919), pages 129–145.
132. CAPART, JEAN. *Les Débuts de l'Art en Egypte.* Vromart, Brussels. 1904.
133. CARTAILHAG and BREUIL. *Les Peintures et Gravures Murales des Cavernes Pyrénéennes, Altamira de Santillane, et Marsoulas.* Masson, Paris. 1905.
134. DEGALLIER, ALICE. "Note Psychologique sur les Négres Pahouins." *Archives de Psychologie*, Vol. 4 (1905), pages 362–368.

170 *Measurement of Intelligence by Drawings*

135. DOEHLEMANN, K. "Prähistorische Kunst und Kinderzeichnungen." *Beiträge zur Anthropologie und Urgeschichte* (1908), page 51.
136. ELLIOTT, G. F. S. *Prehistoric Man and His Story.* London. 1920. (See Chapters 18–19.)
137. GROSSE, ERNST. *The Beginnings of Art.* D. Appleton & Co., New York. 1915.
138. HADDON, A. C. *Evolution in Art.* London. 1895.
139. —— "Drawings by Natives of British New Guinea." *Man*, Vol. 4 (1904), pages 33–36.
140. HOERNES, M. *Urgeschichte der Bildenen Kunst in Europa von den Anfängen bis um 500 vor Christ.* Holzhausen, Vienna. 1898.
141. KOCH-GRÜNBERG, THEODOR. *Anfängen der Kunst im Urwald.* Berlin. 1905.
142. KRETZSCHMAR, JOHANNES. "Kinderkunst und Urzeitkunst." *Zeitschrift für pädagogische Psychologie*, Vol. 11 (1910), pages 354–366.
143. —— "Die Kinderkunst bei den Völkern höherer und niederer Kultur. Ein Beitrag zur vergleichender Pädagogik." *Archiven für Pädagogik*, Vol. 1 (1912), pages 39–61.
144. LAMPRECHT, KARL. "Les Dessins d'Enfants comme Source Historique." *Bulletin de l'Academie Royale de Belgique*, Nos. 9–10, pages 457–469.
145. PROBST, M. "Les Dessins des Enfants Kabyles." *Archives de Psychologie*, Vol. 6 (1906), pages 131–140.
146. ROSEN, FELIX. "Über den Naturalismus der paläolithischen Tierbilder." *Zeitschrift für angewandte Psychologie*, Vol. 4 (1911), pages 556–562.
147. —— "Darstellende Kunst im Kindesalter der Völker." *Zeitschrift für angewandte Psychologie*, Vol. 1 (1908), page 93.
148. RUTTMAN, W. J. "Vergleichende Psychologie der Kinderzeichnungen." *Zeitschrift für pädagogische Psychologie*, Vol. 17 (1916), pages 336–337.
149. SPEARING, H. G. *The Childhood of Art.* G. P. Putnam's Sons, New York. 1913.
150. SPENCER, BALDWIN. *Native Tribes of the Northern Territory of Australia.* The Macmillan Company, New York. 1914. (See Chapter XIV.)
151. STRATZ, C. H. *Darstellung des Menschlichen Körpers.* Berlin. 1914.
152. VAN GENNEP, M. A. "Dessins d'Enfant et Dessin Pre-historique." *Archives de Psychologie*, Vol. 10 (1911), pages 327–337.
153. VERWORN, MAX. "Kinderkunst und Urgeschichte." *Korrespondenz der deutscher anthropologische Gesellschaft* (1907), pages 42–46.
154. VIERKANDT, A. "Das Problem der Felszeichnungen und der Ursprung des Zeichnens." *Archiven für Anthropologie*, Vol. 7 (1919), pages 110–118.
155. —— "Das Zeichnen der Naturvölker." *Zeitschrift für angewandte Psychologie*, Vol. 6 (1912), page 299.

156. WATERMAN, T. T. "Some Conundrums in Northwest Coast Art." *American Anthropologist*, Vol. 25 (1923), pages 435–451.

157. WILSON, T. "Prehistoric Art." *Annual Report of the Board of Regents of the Smithsonian Institution, Report of the United States Natural History Museum* (1896), pages 325–644.

158. WUNDT, WILLIAM. *Elemente der Volkerpsychologie.* Leipzig. 1912. (See also the authorized translation, *Elements of Folk Psychology*, by E. L. Schaub, published by the Macmillan Company, New York, 1916.)

Miscellaneous

159. AYRES, L. P. *Laggards in Our Schools.* Survey Associates, Inc. 112 East 19th Street, New York. 1914. 220 pages.

160. BAGLEY, W. C. "On the Association of Mental with Motor Ability in School Children." *American Journal of Psychology*, Vol. 12 (1901), page 193.

161. BAPPERT, JACOB. "Zur qualitativen Bewertung des Zeichnentests von Binet-Simon." *Zeitschrift für angewandte Psychologie*, Vol. 21 (1923), pages 259–282.

162. BARTLETT, F. C. "The Function of Images." *British Journal of Psychology*, Vol. 11 (1921), pages 320–337.

163. BOOK, WILLIAM F. *Studies in Observational Learning.* Indiana University Publications, Vol. 7, No. 12. 1922. 132 pages.

164. BURT, CYRIL, and MOORE, R. C. "The Mental Differences between the Sexes." *Journal of Experimental Pedagogy*, Vol. 3 (1912), pages 272–284 and 255–388.

165. COHN, J., and DIEFFENBACHER, J. "Untersuchungen über Geschlechts, Alter, und Begabungs-unterschiede bei Schülern." *Zeitschrift für angewandte Psychologie*, Vol. 2 (1911), page 213.

166. DALLENBACH, K. M. "The Effect of Practice upon Visual Apprehension in School Children." *Journal of Experimental Pedagogy*, Vol. 5 (1914), pages 321–334 and 387–404.

167. —— "Effect of Practice upon Visual Apprehension in the Feeble-Minded." *Journal of Educational Psychology*, Vol. 10 (1919), pages 61–82.

168. DESCOUDRES, A. "Couleur, Forme, ou Nombre?" *Archives de Psychologie*, Vol. 14 (1914), pages 305–341.

169. FOSTER, W. S. "The Effect of Practice upon Visualizing and upon the Reproduction of Visual Impressions." *Journal of Educational Psychology*, Vol. 2 (1911), pages 11–21.

170. FRASIER, G. W. "A Comparative Study of the Variability of Boys and Girls." *Journal of Applied Psychology*, Vol. 3 (1919), pages 151–155.

171. GIESE, FRITZ. "Ein Versuch über Gestaltgedächtnis." *Zeitschrift für pädagogische Psychologie*, Vol. 16 (1915), pages 127–131.

172. GRANIT, A. R. "A Study of the Perception of Form." *British Journal of Psychology*, Vol. 12 (1921), pages 223–252.

173. HALL, G. STANLEY. "The Contents of Children's Minds on Entering School." *Pedagogical Seminary*, Vol. 1 (1891), pages 139–173.

174. HOLLINGWORTH, L. S. "Comparison of the Sexes in Mental Traits." *Psychological Bulletin*, Vol. 15 (1918), pages 427–432.

175. KELLEY, TRUMAN L. *Statistical Method.* The Macmillan Company, New York, 1923.

176. KENT, G. H., and ROSANOFF, A. J. "A Study of Association in Insanity." *American Journal of Insanity*, Vol. 67 (1910), pages 37–96 and 317–390.

177. LÉCLÉRE, A. "Description d'un Objet." *L'Année Psychologique*, Vol. 4 (1897), pages 379–389.

178. LURTON, F. E. "Retardation in Fifty-five Western Towns." *Journal of Educational Psychology*, Vol. 3 (1912), pages 242–272.

179. MAURER, L. "Beobachtungen über das Anschauungsvermögen der Kinder." *Zeitschrift für pädagogische Psychologie*, Vol. 5 (1903), pages 62–85.

180. MINNICK, J. H. "A Comparative Study of the Mental Ability of Boys and Girls." *School Review*, Vol. 23 (1915), pages 73–84.

181. MYERS, GARRY C. "A Study in Incidental Memory." *Archives of Psychology*, Vol. 4 (1913), pages 1–108.

182. PARSONS, C. J. "Children's Interpretation of Ink Blots." *British Journal of Psychology*, Vol. 9 (1917), pages 74–92.

183. PHILLIPS, B. A. "Retardation in the Elementary Schools of Philadelphia." *Psychological Clinic*, Vol. 6 (1912), pages 79–90 and 107–121.

184. PORTEUS, S. D. "Sex Differences in Porteus Maze Test Performances." *Training School Bulletin*, Vol. 17 (1920), pages 105–120.

185. PRESSEY, L. W. "Sex Differences Shown by 2544 School Children on a Group Scale of Intelligence, with Special Reference to Variability." *Journal of Applied Psychology*, Vol. 2 (1918), pages 323–340.

186. PRESSEY, S. L. and L. W. "Further Data with Regard to Sex Differences." *Journal of Applied Psychology*, Vol. 5 (1921), pages 78–84.

187. STERN, WILLIAM. "Erinnerung und Aussage in der ersten Kindheit; Ein Kapital aus der Psychogenesis eines Kindes." *Beiträge zur Psychologie der Aussage*, Vol. 2 (1905), pages 32–67.

188. TERMAN, L. M. *The Measurement of Intelligence.* Houghton Mifflin Company, Boston. 1916.

189. —— *The Intelligence of School Children.* Houghton Mifflin Company, Boston. 1919.

190. WEILL, J., and NELLEN, R. "Contribution a l'Étude de la Mémoire des Images chez l'Enfant." *Revue Psychologique*, Vol. 3 (1910), pages 343–348.

191. WHIPPLE, GUY M. "The Effect of Practice upon the Range of Visual Attention and of Visual Apprehension." *Journal of Educational Psychology*, Vol. 1 (1910), pages 249–262.
192. WOOLLEY, HELEN THOMPSON. "The Psychology of Sex." *Psychological Bulletin*, Vol. 11 (1914), pages 353–379.

INDEX

Albien, Gustav, 70

Arms, order of appearance in drawing, 35; constancy of appearance, 75; directions for scoring, 91, 93, 94, 102, 103, 105, 147, 151

Army Alpha Test, 49, 50, 81

Artistic ability, correlation with general ability, 2, 4, 9; effect upon test score, 52, 53, 58

Ayres, L. P., 57

Baldwin, J. M., 1

Ballard, P. B., 15

Barnes, Earl, 1, 2

Bianca, Pamela, 52

Brown, D. D., 1, 8

Burt, Cyril, 5, 76

Cheeks, manner of representing, 145, 147.

Chin, directions for scoring, 108, 109; unusual manner of representing, 139

Claparède, E., 2

Clark, A. B., 1, 72

Classification of drawings, 90, 91

Clothing, directions for scoring, 98, 99; unusual ways of representing, 135, 143, 147

Concept development, indicated by drawings, iii, 12, 72 ff., 82

Cooke, Ebenezer, 1

Correlations, between drawing ability and general ability, 2; between test score and school progress, 24 ff., 49, 50; with other intelligence tests, 50, 51; with teachers' ratings, 50, 52; between masculinity ratings and sex, 59

Crayons, use of, 85, 150, 151

Criteria, used by Ivanoff, 2; for validation of separate points in scale, 14, 17; in selection of subject, 15

Darwin, Charles, 8, 67

Degallier, Alice, 10

Döhleman, K., 10

Drawings, by feeble-minded, 4, 5, 7, 13, 74, 76; by gifted children, 4, 9, 52, 53; by individual children, 8; by prehistoric man, 10, 13; by primitive races, 10, 13, 68; from copy, 12, 72; inaptitude for drawing, 71

Ears, directions for scoring, 106, 107; unusual ways of representing, 135

Erasures, 86, 89

Experience, lack of, 56

Eyes, directions for scoring, 95, 106, 107, 108; unusual ways of representing, 143, 147

Face, special indication of, 131, 149

Feminine characteristics in drawings, 61, 62, 140, 141

Fingers, number drawn, 76, 161; directions for scoring, 100, 101, 127

Forehead, directions for scoring, 108, 109; unusual ways of representing, 139

Fursac, Rogues de, 10, 62

Götze, K., 1

Grade Progress Ratio, 49

Grosse, Ernst, 10

Haddon, A. C., 10

Hair, order of appearance in drawing, 35, 76; directions for scoring, 97, 98; unusual ways of representing, 127, 147

Hamilton, A. M., 10

Hands, directions for scoring, 101

Head, directions for scoring, 91, 105; unusual way of representing, 147

175

$\mathcal{C}$lassics $\mathcal{I}$n

$\mathcal{C}$hild $\mathcal{D}$evelopment

An Arno Press Collection

Baldwin, James Mark. **Thought and Things.** Four vols. in two. 1906-1915

Blatz, W[illiam] E[met], et al. **Collected Studies on the Dionne Quintuplets.** 1937

Bühler, Charlotte. **The First Year of Life.** 1930

Bühler, Karl. **The Mental Development of the Child.** 1930

Claparède, Ed[ouard]. **Experimental Pedagogy and the Psychology of the Child.** 1911

Factors Determining Intellectual Attainment. 1975

First Notes by Observant Parents. 1975

Freud, Anna. **Introduction to the Technic of Child Analysis.** 1928

Gesell, Arnold, et al. **Biographies of Child Development.** 1939

Goodenough, Florence L. **Measurement of Intelligence By Drawings.** 1926

Griffiths, Ruth. **A Study of Imagination in Early Childhood and Its Function in Mental Development.** 1918

Hall, G. Stanley and Some of His Pupils. **Aspects of Child Life and Education.** 1907

Hartshorne, Hugh and Mark May. **Studies in the Nature of Character. Vol. I: Studies in Deceit; Book One, General Methods and Results.** 1928

Hogan, Louise E. **A Study of a Child.** 1898

Hollingworth, Leta S. **Children Above 180 IQ, Stanford Binet:** Origins and Development. 1942

Kluver, Heinrich. **An Experimental Study of the Eidetic Type.** 1926

Lamson, Mary Swift. **Life and Education of Laura Dewey Bridgman, the Deaf, Dumb and Blind Girl.** 1881

Lewis, M[orris] M[ichael]. **Infant Speech:** A Study of the Beginnings of Language. 1936

McGraw, Myrtle B. **Growth: A Study of Johnny and Jimmy.** 1935

Monographs on Infancy. 1975

O'Shea, M. V., editor. **The Child: His Nature and His Needs.** 1925

Perez, Bernard. **The First Three Years of Childhood.** 1888

Romanes, George John. **Mental Evolution in Man:** Origin of Human Faculty. 1889

Shinn, Milicent Washburn. **The Biography of a Baby.** 1900

Stern, William. **Psychology of Early Childhood Up to the Sixth Year of Age.** 1924

Studies of Play. 1975

Terman, Lewis M. **Genius and Stupidity:** A Study of Some of the Intellectual Processes of Seven "Bright" and Seven "Stupid" Boys. 1906

Terman, Lewis M. **The Measurement of Intelligence.** 1916

Thorndike, Edward Lee. **Notes on Child Study.** 1901

Wilson, Louis N., compiler. **Bibliography of Child Study.** 1898-1912

[Witte, Karl Heinrich Gottfried]. **The Education of Karl Witte,** Or the Training of the Child. 1914